CROSSROADS

Approaches in Modern Studies

CHINA
Portrait of a Superpower

Gillian Long

Former Principal Teacher of Modern Studies
Johnstone High School

Vincent Oates

Principal Teacher of Modern Studies
Garnock Academy, Kilbirnie

Blackie

CROSSROADS

GENERAL EDITORS:
Ian Graham and Alex Stirling

ISBN   0 216 91065 X

PUBLISHED BY:
Blackie & Son Ltd
Bishopbriggs, Glasgow G64 2NZ
Furnival House, 14–18 High Holborn, London WC1V 6BX

PRINTED IN GREAT BRITAIN BY:
Thomson Litho Ltd, East Kilbride, Scotland

Preface

CROSSROADS aims to provide a basis for the examination and further study of the underlying and developing influences which affect contemporary institutions, issues and affairs.

The series is designed to meet the needs of school pupils and students in Further Education who are undertaking a course in Modern Studies at the S.C.E. Higher Grade. The texts will also be found useful for those following courses in General Studies for G.C.E.

The subjects covered include industrial organization and development, social change, political parties in Great Britain, race relations, the Great Powers and international relations.

Ian Graham
Alex Stirling
General Editors

Acknowledgments

The authors and publisher would like to thank the following for permission to reproduce copyright material.

John Gittings: page 22
Popperfoto: pages 23, 75, 81
John Hillelson Agency Ltd/Felix Greene: page 25
Bell & Hyman Ltd (from *The Chinese People and the Chinese Earth* by Keith Buchanan): pages 37, 42
Scotland-China Association: page 38
Anglo-Chinese Educational Institute: pages 39, 45, 49, 54, 65, 68

Thanks are also due to Mr Jack Gray for his help in compiling Mao's 'Spiral of Development' on page 14.

Contents

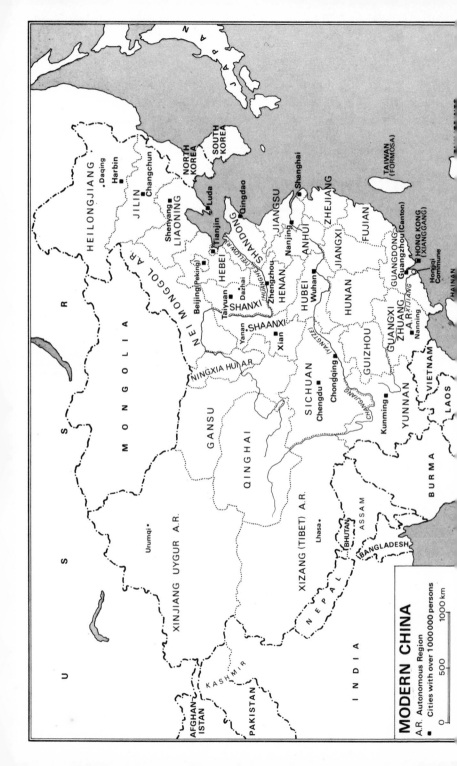

MODERN CHINA

A.R. Autonomous Region
■ Cities with over 1 000 000 persons

0   500   1000 km

Communist China in Perspective

The question 'Why study contemporary China?' is not difficult to answer. China, the third largest country in the world with 1,000 million people, totals one quarter of the world's population. Knowledge of China is not only important in itself but it also enables us to understand world affairs more fully and to make comparisons with other developing countries and other Socialist nations.

But there are a number of factors which make the study of contemporary China particularly challenging. One is our unfamiliarity with the Chinese way of life, with the issues that they see as important and with the way in which their political system dominates most aspects of society. The following extracts from Chinese newspapers describe 'model' citizens who have received national acclaim.

Model worker Shang Guizhen

Shang Guizhen, 29, is a woman worker in the Shanghai Number 14 textile mill and a model worker of the city. 'I'll not marry until I set a record of 600,000 metres of faultless cloth,' she vowed. Three times she persuaded her fiancé to postpone their wedding. Then on 7 December 1979 she made her record-breaking 600,000 metres. At their wedding, leading cadres and workers of her mill went to congratulate the bride and the groom. 'I'm determined to try for another record in 1980,' said Shang, 'and play my part in China's Socialist modernization.'

Model pig-raiser elected to Provincial Party Congress

Zhou Longdi, 44, is a model pig-raiser. She receives praise

from all the members of her commune. Although she has heavy household chores and does not keep well, she decided to raise pigs despite the fact that pig-breeding is dirty and tiresome. As a result of Zhou's care there are now hundreds of hogs and dozens of sows on the brigade's farm. When asked why she raised pigs of her own accord she said, 'As a Party member I ought to shoulder the heaviest burden.' In 1980 she was elected to the Jiangsu Provincial Party Congress.

Li Weihan, a veteran revolutionary, recalls his 60 years' experience

'A communist must have lofty ideals and an unbending spirit. He should be able to stand the tests of hard struggle as well as the tests after victory has been won. He should forever maintain the revolutionary spirit and work whole-heartedly for the benefit of the people. In this respect Comrades Mao Zedong (Mao Tse-tung)[1] and Zhou Enlai (Chou En-lai) are our guides. We should hand down the Party's fine tradition and style of work from generation to generation so as to build China into a strong and modern Socialist country.'

Not only is Chinese society very different from our own but it is also one in which change is a keynote. Whilst 1949 saw the beginning of Communist rule, it by no means marked the end of the revolution. To western observers the Chinese political scene is often confusing; leading figures fall from favour and apparently sharp shifts in policy are made. A knowledge of the political background to these changes is all-important both to any study of contemporary China and to an understanding of future events. Chapter 2 tries to provide this political context. It is vital to remember that the Chinese themselves view their own society as a developing one.

Precisely because this short book concentrates on con-temporary China, little attempt has been made to explain events prior to 1949. Nevertheless we begin with a brief historical sketch of the rise to power of the Communist Party of China.

China's social structure changed little until the beginning of the twentieth century. For centuries the Emperor was a supreme autocrat who ruled his vast territories with the aid of an élite of nobles and scholar-officials. Below them were the uneducated and underprivileged masses, most of whom were poor peasants. Rarely a year went by without uprisings against the government taking place. Until the nineteenth century China isolated herself from the West, whose traditions she regarded as barbaric and inferior to her own. Indeed the word 'China' means 'centre of the world' or 'middle kingdom'. Colonial expansion in the nineteenth century broke through this barrier and opened China to foreign exploitation. An important result of this was the rapid spread of new political ideas such as Democracy, Liberalism and Communism. Many Chinese students educated abroad returned home highly critical of the corrupt and inefficient Manchu regime.

In 1911 a revolution led by the western-educated Dr Sun Yat-sen finally overthrew the imperial system and established a republic. Thereafter, conflict in China was endemic. That conflict ended on 1 October 1949 when Mao Zedong, Chairman of the Communist Party of China (C.P.C.), declared the establishment of the People's Republic of China (P.R.C.).

THE RISE TO POWER OF THE COMMUNIST PARTY OF CHINA

The C.P.C., established in 1921 in Shanghai, was born into a confused political situation in which the major contestant for power was the Kuomintang or Nationalist Party. From 1927 Communism was outlawed and, under the leadership of Chiang Kai-shek, the Kuomintang (K.M.T.) sought to eliminate Communist opposition. Forced to retreat to rural mountain areas, the C.P.C. abandoned the idea of a revolution led by the urban working class and, by establishing independent governments, called soviets, built its organization on peasant support.

The Japanese invasion of Manchuria in 1931 and subsequent occupation of China during the Second World

War brought a temporary halt to the civil war between the C.P.C. and the K.M.T., forcing them to join in an 'Anti-Japanese United Front'. In 1945 civil war recommenced, but by then the Communists enjoyed widespread popular support. Many of Chiang's own generals willingly joined in the final operation which drove their leader and the remnants of the K.M.T. to exile in Formosa.

There were two main factors behind the Communists' rise to power. Firstly, China's large population, dominated by a small land-owning class, was overwhelmingly poor. The C.P.C. programme of land redistribution and fair taxation offered relief from the oppression of the landlord and from crippling K.M.T. taxes. The experience of the soviets contrasted sharply with the corrupt and despotic Nationalist regime. For tens of thousands of peasants, Communist rule substantially improved their way of life.

Secondly, the Communists also appealed to the strong nationalist feelings of the Chinese. As the proponent of the 'United Front', the C.P.C. compromised its own political programme and accepted Chiang's leadership in the war against Japan. Communist guerrilla tactics proved much more successful than the traditional manoeuvres employed by Chiang's armies, and behind Japanese lines enthusiastic cadres spread the Communist message. The lack of corruption in Communist-controlled areas and the considerate behaviour of the Red Army were also important factors in the growth of Communist support.

The party that Mao led to power contained many of the people that were later to become famous in Communist China, like Lin Biao (Lin Piao), Zhou Enlai, Zhu De (Chu Teh), Deng Xiaoping (Teng Hsiao-ping) and Liu Shaoqi (Liu Shao-chi). With Mao they had undergone extreme hardships to ensure a Communist victory, but although firmly committed to Marxist ideals, they had their own ideas as to how to achieve a Communist society.

A summary of problems and progress 1949–66

Rural poverty was a most pressing problem. In 1949, according to official Chinese estimates, poor and middle peasants, 90% of the population, owned only 30% of the land. The remaining 70% was owned and rented out by rich peasants and landlords. Extortionate rents and high taxation forced many peasants into debt and starvation.

The following extracts give an insight into the poverty of peasant life before 1949.

Intolerable taxes are nothing new in China, but they pale into ... insignificance before the regime of Chiang Kai-shek ... From 1929 to 1933 there were 188 different kinds of taxes ... Far worse than the formal land tax, however, were the surtaxes which were usually ten times the principal tax ... In Sichuan province ... sometimes as much as fifty-nine per cent of the crop per mow of paddy field was taken by the tax collectors. [In many places] where tenants formerly gave half of their rice or wheat crop to the landlord they now had to give seventy, eighty or ninety per cent of that crop. Sometimes, as I discovered on the Chengdu Plain, it was over 100 per cent, so that the tenant had to go out and buy rice to meet his taxes. In other words he might work all year in his paddy fields and yet not have 1 grain of rice for himself.[2]

There were 3 famines in a row. The whole family went out to beg things to eat. Conditions were very bad. Many mothers threw newborn children in the river. We had to sell our eldest daughter.
We sold what few things we had, ... took our patched quilt ... and set out ... On the fourth morning [a] woman said she wanted to buy [our son]. We put him on the kang [heated platform]. He fell asleep. In the next room we were paid 5 silver dollars [£1]. Then they drove us out. My heart was so bitter. We wept all day on the road.
During the famine we ate leaves and the remnants from the vinegar making. We were so weak and hungry we could not walk. I went out to the hills to get leaves and there the people were fighting each other over the leaves on the trees. My little sister starved to death. My brother's wife could not bear the hunger and ran away ... My cousin was forced to become a landlord's concubine.[3]

	1949	1952	1957	1965	1970	1976	1979	1981†
G.N.P. (b. 1976 U.S. $)	—	87	112	165	231	324	—	—
Population (m.)	540	570	640	750	840	951	971*	—
Per capita G.N.P. (1976 U.S. $)	—	153	190	220	275	340	—	—
Membership of C.P.C. (m.)	4·5*	—	11·5*	—	—	—	38·5*	—
Number of Industrial Workers (m.)	8*	—	24·5*	—	—	—	74·5*	—
Agriculture								
Agricultural Production Index (1957 = 100)	54	83	100	104	127	148	—	—
Total Grain (m. metric tonnes)	111	161	191	194	243	285	332*	343*
Cotton (m. metric tonnes)	0·4	1·3	1·6	1·9	2	2·3	2·6*	2·55*
Hogs (m. of head)	58	58	115	168	226	280	319*	—
Draft Animals (m. of head)	60	—	83	—	94	—	94·5*	—
Industry								
Industrial Production Index (1957 = 100)	20	48	100	199	316	502	614*	—
Electric Power (b. kWh)	—	7·3	19·3	42	72	—	282*	312*
Coal (m. metric tonnes)	—	66·5	130·7	220	310	448	635*	620*
Crude Oil (m. metric tonnes)	—	0·4	1·5	11	28·2	83·6	106·1*	106·1*
Crude Steel (m. metric tonnes)	—	1·3	5·4	12·5	17·8	23	32·9*	35*
Chemical Fertilizer (m. metric tonnes)	—	0·2	0·8	7·6	14	—	—	—
Cement (m. metric tonnes)	—	2·9	6·9	16·3	26·6	49·3	73·9*	78*
Timber (m. cubic metres)	5·6*	11·2*	—	—	—	—	54·4*	49·1*

Machinery Index (1957 = 100)	—	33	100	257	587	—	—
Electric Generators (m. kW)	—	—	0·3	0·8	—	190·9	—
Tractors (th. 15 h.p. units)	—	—	23·9	79	190·9	—	—
Trucks (th. units)	—	7·5	30	70	—	—	—
Locomotives (units)	20	167	50	435	—	—	—
Consumer Goods Index (1957 = 100)	60	100	183	272	—	573·3*	—
Bicycles (m.)	0·1	0·8	1·8	3·6	—	10·09*	14·84*
Televisions (m.)	—	—	—	—	—	1·3*	—
Radios (m.)	—	—	—	—	—	13·8*	—
Exports (b. 1976 U.S. $)	0·4	0·9	1·6	2	—	6·9	13·5
Imports (b. 1976 U.S. $)	0·4	1	1·4	1·8	2·2	6	14·5
Education							
% Population Illiterate	85*	40*	—	25*	—	—	—
Primary School Students (m.)	24*	51*	64*	116*	150*	149*	—
Middle School Students (m.)	1·26*	3·1*	7*	14·4*	45*	59*	—
University/College Students (th.)	117*	191*	444*	674*	500*	600*	600*
Health							
Health Workers (m.)	0·078*	1·9*	—	—	—	2·6*	—

NOTE: † = projected, b. = billions, m. = millions, th. = thousands

Table 1.1 Selected economic indicators. * indicates official Chinese figures; all other figures are from western sources. Because of China's size, the lack of proper and comprehensive statistical methods and political bias, all figures should be used with caution. Their main value is that they indicate general trends.

With the passing of the Agrarian Reform Law in 1950, land, animals and possessions were taken from the land-owning classes and redistributed amongst the peasantry. The land reform movement strengthened support for the Party. By 1952 the C.P.C. was indisputably in control; cadres filled all the important posts, political study was stressed, and propaganda campaigns extolling Communist virtues were launched through the State-controlled mass media.

The C.P.C. saw collectivization as the basis for the introduction of scientific farming. In 1951 Mutual Aid teams were established; land was privately owned but peasants were encouraged to pool their animals and tools to achieve higher yields. The lower stage co-operatives in which several teams combined to sow and harvest their crops, appeared between 1955 and 1956 and were closely followed by higher stage 'Advanced Co-operatives'. In these, private ownership of land, apart from a small vegetable plot, was abandoned and peasants were paid for the work done. The final stage of collectivization, in 1958, established the 'People's Communes', much larger units which today combine economic with political and social functions.

In 1949 the Communists inherited little industry. In the coastal cities there were some light industries, many of which were foreign-owned. The only heavy industry, a legacy of the Japanese, was located in Manchuria. An important effect of the years of colonial domination was that there were few Chinese with any industrial or managerial expertise. The leadership of the Party itself had gained most of its experience in the rural areas. A programme of gradual nationalization brought all in-dustries, commerce and banking under State control and in the Five-Year Plans, introduced in 1952 and 1957, industrialization was given priority. The Sino-Soviet treaty signed in 1950 brought Russian finance and technical aid to create the heavy industrial base necessary for China's economic expansion.

As reference to the statistical table shows, by the mid-1960s substantial progress had been made, not only in agricultural and industrial production, but also in the fields of health, education and welfare. Formal education had expanded, the illiteracy rate had dropped considerably and health services existed where there had been none before. Huge problems still remained, but for the first time in centuries China had a strong central government which had brought about a measure of social justice. On the eve of the Cultural Revolution in 1966 the majority of Chinese citizens undoubtedly enjoyed a higher standard of living than at any previous time in their history.

---

[1] All Chinese words are spelt according to the recently introduced Chinese phonetic system. In important instances the former spelling appears in brackets.

[2] *China Shakes the World* J. Belden (PELICAN, 1973).

[3] *Fanshen: Documentary of Revolution in a Chinese Village* W. Hinton (MONTHLY REVIEW PRESS, 1980).

Ideology and Leaders 1949–80

COMMUNIST IDEOLOGY

Although China's leaders would support the slogans 'Ideology is the guiding light' and 'Politics must be in command', it would be wrong to assume that they have always been in agreement over the interpretation of ideology or the practical policies that should be followed to achieve their aim of a classless society. Since 1921 frequent leadership struggles, reflecting different ideological and practical viewpoints, have taken place within the C.P.C.; central to these struggles have been the influence and ideas of Mao Zedong. China's present leaders clearly have their own political and economic priorities but these can only be understood by examining previous intra-party conflicts

All Communists accept the theories of Marx and Lenin as the foundation of their ideology. Marx analysed history in terms of class struggle—the struggle of one class against another for control of the economic base of society. Writing in the nineteenth century in a Europe dominated by Capitalism, Marx envisaged a final revolution in which the urban working class (proletariat) would overthrow the bourgeois and Capitalist classes (the owners of the means of production). Communism, a classless society, would be achieved when there was sufficient wealth for 'each according to his needs'. Both Marx and Lenin saw Socialism as the transition period before Communism. In this period the 'dictatorship of the proletariat' would be achieved under Communist party leadership. In their theories, Marx and Lenin stressed the role of the proletariat; they paid little attention to the revolutionary potential of the peasantry.

The Soviet model of development

Ironically enough the first Communist revolution in 1917, although won on the basis of urban support, occurred in a poor and largely peasant country. It was in Russia that Marxism-Leninism, as interpreted by Stalin, was first implemented on a national scale.

The Soviet model of development took industrialization as the key. Massive investments were made in heavy industry to bring about the rapid industrialization of the economy. It was accepted that, initially, agriculture would provide the bulk of the funds for industry which, once developed, would bring about the mechanization of farming. Central planning and incentive wage schemes were important features of this model. Under the National Five-Year Plans every economic enterprise was given output targets, and bonus payments were linked to increases in production. In education, great stress was placed on the creation of an élite of skilled workers and specialists whose expertise was essential to the industrialization programme. The model embodied the ideal of an urban society, demanding the proletarianization and urbanization of the population.

In implementing this model the Communist Party of the Soviet Union (C.P.S.U.) relied heavily on disciplined Party members who unquestioningly carried out the decisions of their leaders.

It was this model of development that China adopted in 1949. Why was this? It must be remembered that the Soviet Union was the first and most powerful Communist country and was recognized as leader of the Communist world by the C.P.C. leaders, many of whom had trained in Russia. Faced with the awesome problem of governing China in 1949, they saw the 'advanced experience of the Soviet Union' as the fastest way of achieving economic progress. Moreover, the acceptance of the Soviet approach guaranteed the Chinese large amounts of financial and practical help.

MAOISM

In 1949, as Chairman of the C.P.C., Mao was clearly a willing party to the implementation of the Soviet model in China. However, by the mid-1950s he was beginning to voice criticisms of China's progress. He proposed an alternative model of development based on his own philosophy and revolutionary experience.

Born in 1893, in Hunan, into a poor peasant family, Mao was a founder member of the C.P.C. in 1921. A committed Marxist, he sought to apply Marxism to China. In 1927, faced with the reality of the situation, he had said:

> In a very short time ... several hundred million peasants will rise like a mighty storm ... We can ... lead them, trail behind them or oppose them ...

In favouring the first course, Mao recognized the revolutionary potential of the peasantry and in doing so first departed from orthodox Marxism. Time was to prove his approach correct. In China the proletariat was numerically insignificant and it was amongst the peasantry in the 1930s and 1940s that Communism grew. Mao saw the peasantry as the basis for a Socialist society. From 1937 to 1942 in the Yanan (Yenan) soviet, an extremely poor region in north west China, he tested many of his ideas. His approach, designed to consolidate support for the C.P.C., was arguably the most important reason for the Communists' success in 1949.

Mao's political model—the 'Mass Line'

Mao's theory of the 'Mass Line' concerned the style of leadership and the relationship of the Party with the masses. Mao believed in a strong, highly-disciplined Party, one that was responsive to the masses and accountable for its actions:

> All correct leadership is necessarily from the masses to the masses. This means: take the ideas of the masses (scattered and unsystematic) and concentrate them (through study turn them into concentrated and system-

atic ideas) then go to the masses and propagate and explain these ideas until the masses embrace them as their own. (1943)

Mao envisaged a continuing dialogue between the leadership and the led. This would strengthen loyalty to the C.P.C. and simultaneously combat the growth of dogmatism and bureaucratism within the Party, and the imposition of policies irrelevant to peasant needs.

In practice, in Yanan, considerable stress was placed on political study. Cadres were required to take part in manual labour and to subject themselves and their policies to criticism from the masses.

Mao's economic model

With its infertile soils, a poverty-stricken and scattered population of 5 million and an almost total lack of industry, the Yanan region offered little scope for economic advance. Here, under constant enemy attack and without external aid, development was, of necessity, based on existing resources.

Mao argued that the only resource that China had in abundance was labour and it was this that had to fund agricultural development. Mao's model saw a self-sufficient community as the ideal. To this end it demanded the exploitation of all existing resources by the community itself.

A group of peasants had first to employ themselves on a given project, for example by co-operating in the building of a small dam to provide irrigation for their crops. This would involve the use of labour and simple tools—carrying-poles, baskets and shovels. If successful, the project would achieve an increase in agricultural production, providing the peasants with additional income and the incentive for further development. Part of the profit from the venture would be re-invested, for example to purchase better tools for making dam construction easier or for use in alternative projects. And so, over a considerable period of time, by accumulating and re-investing profits, development would spiral. The government would encourage this by a low

13

Over a long period of time this will result in the creation of a flourishing rural community and a gradual rise in individual incomes.

Richer commune and richer peasants = demand for industrial goods which means a boost to the industrial sector. But industry must be geared to agricultural needs.

Investment in better tools and equipment for construction, mechanization or side-line projects.

Political demands. Peasant commitment to communal activity = willingness to re-invest. Local initiative and autonomy in decision-making. Good local leadership. Low taxation policy for rural sector.

Greater profit for the commune = higher income for the peasants and the possibility of re-investment.

Better irrigation = increase in agricultural production.

Peasants combine to undertake a construction project e.g. a small irrigation dam. This requires basic tools and labour.

Large number of peasants = labour surplus, especially in the slack season.

Mao's 'spiral of development'.

taxation policy, in the hope that peasant conservatism towards new methods and co-operative effort would wane as their livelihood improved.

Mao urged that the peasants should invest their limited funds in small projects like labour-intensive industries and intermediate technology (simple machinery). In the long term, Mao hoped that industry would benefit in two ways. Firstly, increased agricultural production would provide greater funds for industrial development. Secondly, the increases would both stimulate demand for agricultural mechanization and provide the peasants with the means to buy the new machinery.

Co-operative effort and a 'Mass Line' style of leadership were essential parts of Mao's economic model. Without the willing participation of the peasants and sensitive direction by the cadres, the economic spiral could not have been sustained.

Mao's social model

Mao's model required that education, health and culture should also serve peasant needs and aid agricultural progress. In Yanan, the stress on local development resulted in an education system which provided mass literacy programmes and practical courses in schools managed and financed by the peasants themselves (mass-run schools). Medical personnel with a very basic training, later known as 'barefoot doctors', concentrated on the treatment of common ailments and improvement in public hygiene and peasant diet.

All books and films carried a political message. Drama troupes and travelling cinemas visited isolated villages urging co-operative effort, hard work and loyalty to the C.P.C.

THE GREAT LEAP FORWARD

In 1945 at their seventh congress, the C.P.C. claimed the 'Thought of Mao Zedong is our sole guide'. However, at the eighth congress in 1956 only Marx and Lenin were extolled; any reference to Mao was omitted. The declining influence of Mao's views coincided with his increasing criticism during the 1950s of the Soviet model, which he claimed was politically and economically unsuited to the needs of China's massive peasant population.

In Mao's view the over-concentration on heavy industry in the years 1950–6 had resulted in the neglect of agriculture. He argued that the over-taxing of the peasantry had led to a decline in agricultural investment. Industry had not produced the machinery and fertilizers crucial for the modernization of farming. Mao pointed to the 1953 census which showed a large percentage of rural unemployment as evidence of the widening material gap between rural peasants and urban workers. Similarly, educational, cultural and health services were most evident in the urban areas and little attention was paid to the Yanan experience. Most dangerous of all, in Mao's view, was the appearance of élitist and dogmatic views of a Soviet type within the Party bureaucracy. The message for Mao was clear—to continue the Soviet approach would be to risk alienating the peasant support on which the C.P.C. depended.

In a speech 'On the Correct Handling of Contradictions among the People' (1957), Mao expressed the idea that under Socialism and even under Communism there would continue to be contradictions. He defined contradictions as conflict between different groups in society. In pre-Communist society, contradictions were antagonistic—the class struggle between workers and peasants and the exploiting Capitalist classes. Under Socialism, Mao maintained that contradictions were mainly non-antagonistic; he instanced the conflict of interests between the leadership and the led. He expressed his fear that élitist and bureaucratic tendencies amongst the Party cadres and intellectuals could produce a class antagonistic to workers and peasants. He maintained that if Socialism were to be achieved, non-antagonistic contradictions had to be resolved, by continuing the class struggle and waging ideological revolution.

It will take a considerable time to decide the issue in the ideological struggle between Socialism and Capitalism in our country. This is because the influence of the bourgeoisie and intellectuals ... will remain as the ideology of a class for a long time to come ... There has been a falling off recently in ideological and political work ... some people apparently think that there is no longer any need to concern themselves with politics ...

In 1958 Mao launched the Great Leap Forward (G.L.F.), his first attempt to radically alter the course of Socialist development. Stuart Schram, an eminent Sinologist, has described this as Mao's effort to 'universalize the Yanan experience'.

In the G.L.F., agricultural development was given top priority and light and heavy industry were geared to meet agricultural needs. The most significant development was the spread of rural communes, in which private plots and sideline activities were discouraged and small industries such as 'back yard furnaces' mushroomed. In order to give greater scope to local initiative, decision-making was decentralized and cadres were sent to the countryside to work. Other features of communization were the introduction of 'barefoot doctors' and the expansion of mass-run schools. In the formal full-time system a new stress was placed on political study. China's intellectuals had to be 'red', i.e. followers of Communism as well as 'expert'.

The Great Leap Forward encountered severe difficulties from the start. Ineffective leadership and peasant opposition to communization hampered agricultural advance. The economy was severely damaged by a series of natural disasters, and food shortages were widespread. In 1960, the sudden withdrawal of Soviet aid dealt a crippling blow to China's industry.

The 'Two Road Struggle'

Apart from these very practical reasons for the failure of the G.L.F., more serious for Mao was the opposition he encountered within the leadership of the C.P.C. From the early 1960s, a bitter intra-party conflict developed, now known as the 'Two Road Struggle', which culminated in the Great Proletarian Cultural Revolution in 1966.

In 1959 Mao resigned as Chairman of the P.R.C., and his place was taken by Liu Shaoqi. It was Liu and Deng Xiaoping who were most closely associated with the anti-Maoist elements within the leadership and who were responsible for the policies implemented after 1960, many of which contradicted the Great Leap Forward. Mao was later to castigate them as 'revisionists' for their alleged pro-Soviet leanings.

In agriculture, private plots were once again permitted and small local industries declined. Economically the balance swung back to heavy industry. In education, the creation of special schools for gifted children demonstrated the renewed status given to academic excellence; political study was paid less attention. The new educational élite were to be 'experts' first and 'red' second. Although lip service continued to be paid to the 'Mass Line', less emphasis was placed on cadre involvement in manual labour. Mao believed that the continuation of these policies would be fatal to Socialism in China. He moved to eliminate the opposition within the Party.

In 1960 Mao began to seek support outwith the C.P.C. by initiating a campaign to turn the People's Liberation Army (P.L.A) into a 'school of Mao Zedong Thought'. For instance, soldiers were expected to engage in intensive study of Mao's works and to spread the Maoist message by working alongside the workers and the peasants. In 1962 the Socialist Education Campaign was launched to combat élitism and bureaucracy within the Party. Mao used the campaign to direct the ideological debate. He warned, 'Never forget class struggle'. The following year Mao stated that unless the Party was reformed it would 'undoubtedly become a fascist party and the whole of China would change its colour ...'. The P.L.A. published the first edition of *Quotes from Chairman Mao* in 1964, and in the following January Mao confronted his high-level opponents within the leadership. He referred to them as 'those in authority who are taking the Capitalist road'. By now Mao was convinced that the Party bureaucrats and officials were a class antagonistic to the workers and peasants. In 1966 he launched the Cultural Revolution.

THE GREAT PROLETARIAN CULTURAL REVOLUTION 1966-8

In August 1966 the 'Sixteen Points' were published, clearly stating the objectives of the revolution: 'to struggle against and overthrow those persons in authority who are taking the Capitalist road, to criticize and repudiate the reactionary bourgeois academic authorities and to transform education, literature and art'.

By calling on China's students and activists to 'repudiate revisionism', Mao was attempting to mobilize youthful ideological fervour and 'to cultivate a generation of revolutionary successors' who would secure Mao's brand of Socialism in China. Young people formed into bands of 'Red Guards' under such slogans as 'We are the critics of the old world and the builders of the new', and 'Forever the guardians of Mao Zedong Thought'.

The 'Red Guard' movement spread rapidly. In all parts of China, Party cadres and State officials suspected of being anti-Maoist were attacked and criticized. Here is one account of a meeting in which Wang Guangmei, wife of Liu Shaoqi, and herself a leading cadre, was criticized.

The accuser listed many of Wang's crimes. She had deliberately [belittled] leading cadres whilst shielding landlords and rich peasants. She had shunned physical labour and refused to practise the three togethers with the peasants—eat together, work together, live together ... She acted not at all like a proletarian cadre ... but a Capitalist class-stinking lady.[1]

Teachers and others in positions of authority who symbolized the bourgeois ideals of the 'old' society were also attacked and often subjected to violence. Ken Ling remembers:

... rows of teachers ... with black ink poured over their heads and faces ... Hanging on their necks were placards with such words as 'reactionary academic authority so and so, class enemy so and so, capitalist roader' ... I saw the principal, the pail around his neck was so heavy the wire had cut deep into his neck ... Finally they all knelt down ... and begged Mao Zedong to pardon their crimes.[1]

The following criticism of a provincial Party Secretary appeared in the People's Daily *in 1967.*

He was arrogant and dogmatic; he refused to discuss things with the masses and ignored the teachings of our great leader Chairman Mao; he corruptly used his high influence to secure 'backdoor entry' into the best schools in Xian for his children and he ignored the needs of the people and betrayed the Party by buying expensive works of art and hoarding grain in his house.

Red Guard activity took place on such a massive scale that China became almost ungovernable. In July 1967 Mao called in the army to restore order.

What had Mao gained from the Cultural Revolution? Within the leadership his chief opponents had been eliminated. Liu Shaoqi, accused of being the 'arch Capitalist roader' and 'China's Khrushchev', was dismissed, rendered 'politically dead' and ultimately expelled from the Party. He died, still in disgrace, in 1969. Deng Xiaoping was also criticized and sent to reform through labour. This practice, known as 'remoulding', was the fate of cadres with suspect ideology. Many were required to attend 'May 7th' schools where intensive political education was combined with physical labour. Although Party organization had been destroyed, after 1968 it was gradually rebuilt. Revolutionary Committees, the new organs of government, composed of representatives from the Party, the army and the masses, appeared at every level of authority, in every institution, commune, factory and school. These extremely powerful committees were the means by which Maoist policy was implemented after 1968.

Perhaps the overwhelming result of the Cultural Revolution was the deification of Mao himself. The *Thoughts of Mao Zedong* became the people's bible. Under the popular slogan 'politics in command', Maoism now dominated economic, political, social and cultural activity.

The power struggle 1976

From the time of the Cultural Revolution until the death of Mao in 1976, there were few public disputes within the leadership. The most serious threat to Mao's supremacy was the alleged attempted coup by Lin Biao, Mao's 'comrade in arms', chosen successor and leader of the P.L.A. He was killed in 1971 whilst attempting to escape to the Soviet Union.

The strength of Mao's personality undoubtedly maintained unity in the ranks, but towards the end of his life factions began to emerge in preparation for the forthcoming struggle. In this context the death of Zhou Enlai, in January 1976, was of crucial importance. From 1949 Zhou had been China's Premier and chief administrator. He had always supported Mao and it was largely due to his efforts that China's economy and administration had not totally collapsed during the Cultural Revolution. In April 1976 Hua Guofeng succeeded Zhou, becoming acting Premier.

Chairman Mao was deeply mourned by the Chinese people when he died in September 1976 but at the political level the power struggle broke out in earnest. Hua assumed the Chairmanship of the Party in October 1976 and moved quickly to silence opponents. Curiously enough the main opposition group, later known as the 'Gang of Four', was led by Mao's widow Jiang Qing (Chiang Ching).

THE 'GANG OF FOUR'

Although usually labelled 'extreme Maoists', it is difficult to determine the relationship between the Gang and Mao, and the exact nature of the policies they favoured. The evidence is highly coloured by the present leadership's total condemnation of the Gang.

Certainly, after 1968, Madame Mao was in firm control of China's mass media. Under her direction all western and much traditional Chinese culture disappeared, and was replaced by highly political dramas known as 'revolutionary operas'.

We know that the Gang were fervently anti-élitist and supporters of radical educational reforms, the abolition of private plots and the end of all incentive wage schemes. For the Gang, 'left' political attitudes were essential; 'redness' was more important than expertise or increased production.

Support for the Gang was mostly in the urban areas where, in preparation for the forthcoming struggle, they had armed some local militias. However, in October 1976, supported by the army and the majority of the Party, Hua Guofeng had little difficulty in ordering their arrest. The Gang were officially charged with counter-revolutionary activities and seeking power for their own aggrandizement.

THE NEW LEADERSHIP

The eleventh Party Congress held in July 1977 officially marked the change in leadership. Hua Guofeng was elected as Chairman and Deng Xiaoping was reinstated in the Party hierarchy.

Between 1977 and 1979 the joint leadership pursued two major policies: the 'Four Modernizations' and the 'Campaign to criticize Lin Biao and the "Gang of Four"'. The 'Four Modernizations' is a national campaign for modern agriculture, industry, science and technology and national defence. In order to fulfil its aim of making China a modern industrial country by the year 2000, the leadership has introduced a number of important changes, which will be discussed in later chapters.

The 'Four Modernizations' are promoted in a roadside poster.

The iron fist of the Party smashes the 'Gang of Four'.

In the 'Campaign of criticism', which was officially concluded in 1979, Lin Biao and the 'Gang of Four' were jointly accused of having followed ultra-leftist policies which, in the post-Cultural Revolution years, led to widespread economic and political chaos.

In particular, the Gang were charged with having magnified the need for class struggle, having wrongfully attacked and persecuted leading Party members and having severely damaged the credibility and authority of the Party. The leadership claimed that the Gang's ultra-egalitarian economic policies and attempts to level wage differentials had led to a dramatic drop in production. Moreover, the Gang's aim of 'national self-sufficiency' had ignored 'learning from foreign countries', which, as we shall see, is a vital element in present economic policy.

Jiang Qing's educational and cultural policies were criticized because, it was claimed, they had prevented free expression in literature, music and art, and had halted educational progress and scientific research by condemning many intellectuals to 'reform through labour'.

Not least, the Gang were said to have 'wilfully distorted Chairman Mao's Thought', but it is clear that even in those early days some attacks on the Gang were also

23

criticisms of Mao. The point of the intensive propaganda against the Gang was to show the Chinese people the 'new' lines of thinking.

The approach of the new leadership is essentially practical and pragmatic; revolutionary politics must come second: 'Modernization is the central task of the Party. There will be no more political movements or class struggles which deviate from this central task and are detrimental to modernization.' (*Beijing Review*, 1979) After the eleventh Party Congress, much effort was expended on re-establishing Party control and a number of important figures who were previously associated with Maoist policies disappeared from the political scene and were replaced by cadres who were disgraced during and after the Cultural Revolution. Many of these people who have been re-habilitated have the administrative skills and expertise vital to China's economic programme.

However, in 1980 cracks began to appear in the façade of Party unity, and a number of important events signified a deepening rift between Hua and Deng. This is perhaps not so surprising when we consider the background of these two men.

Hua Guofeng became a leading cadre in the province of Hunan during the Great Leap Forward. A supporter of the commune movement, he achieved the rank of Provincial Party Secretary in 1959. During the Cultural Revolution, Hua escaped criticism and in 1971 he was transferred to Beijing to serve under Zhou Enlai in the Ministries of Agriculture and National Security. His record, particularly the fact that he worked in the areas of agriculture, education and culture, suggests a man very much in the Maoist mould. Indeed, it is claimed that shortly before his death, Mao designated Hua as his successor. Mao is reported as having said, 'With you in charge I am at ease.'

Deng Xiaoping has a very different history, and although as Vice-Chairman of the Party, Deng is theoretically second to Hua, he is undoubtedly the most important man in China today. Disgraced in 1967 and again in 1976 when he was attacked by Jiang Qing as an 'unrepentant Capitalist roader', Deng has twice risen from 'political death'. His restoration in 1977 underlines the fact that he enjoys considerable support within the Party, the army and the bureaucracy. Once quoted as saying, 'Who cares whether some people are not "red" or politically pure as long as they do a decent job to help modernize China', it is Deng's firm commitment to the modernization programme and pragmatic policies which carry the day.

Many of the cadres recently returned to positions of power share Deng's experience of political exile and his views. It is a measure of his support that Party history is now being re-assessed. References are now made to the mistakes made in 1958 during the Great Leap Forward and a leading article published in 1980 dismissed the 'Two Road Struggle' as fictitious. The Cultural Revolution itself is directly under attack. In a recent speech Vice-Chairman Ye Jianying said:

> When the Cultural Revolution was launched the estimate made of the situation within the Party ... ran counter to reality, no accurate definition of revisionism was given and an erroneous policy and method of struggle were adopted, deviating from the principle of democratic centralism.

'With you in charge I am at ease'. Chairman Mao and Hua Guofeng in 1976.

Confirmation of this view was provided in spring 1980 by the posthumous rehabilitation of Liu Shaoqi, once re-garded as the chief 'Capitalist roader'. In a speech at a memorial meeting held in honour of Liu, Deng said: 'There never was a counter-revolutionary line represented by Comrade Liu Shaoqi'. The years 1968–76 are now viewed as having been a disastrous period. Deng and his supporters claim that the chaos and economic malaise produced by the Cultural Revolution amply justify their new policies.

The resignation of Hua as Premier in September 1980 and the appointment of Zhao Ziyang can be viewed as a victory for the pragmatists and a clear indication that Deng intends his modernization programme to remain Party policy. Zhao not only has the key qualification of having been disgraced during the Cultural Revolution, but since 1975 he has worked in Sichuan, China's most populous province, introducing economic measures which, as we shall see, form a central part of today's policies. It is Zhao's success in raising production which accounts for his rapid rise to the Premiership.

However, we should not regard this as the final word. The speed with which the political scene moves calls into question both the future of Chairman Hua and the relevance of Mao in China today, a discussion of which is left until Chapter 6. One point on which Hua and Deng clearly agree is the need to maintain and strengthen the role of the Communist Party, and it is to this subject that we now turn.

---

[1] *Red Guard Schoolboy to 'Little General' in Mao's China* K. Ling (MACDONALD, 1972)

Party, State and Individual

The People's Republic of China is a Socialist State of the dictatorship of the proletariat led by the working class and based on the alliance of the workers and peasants. The working class exercises leadership over the State through its vanguard the C.P.C. The State adheres to the principle of democracy and ensures to the people the right to participate in the management of State affairs and of all economic and cultural undertakings and the right to supervise State organs and their personnel. (State Constitution, 1978)

Both the theory and practice of Socialist democracy differ greatly from Capitalist democracy in the western sense. In Britain, for example, democracy is characterized by representative government chosen by an electoral process in which several parties take part, by an independent legal system, and by individual rights such as freedom of expression and organization. The Chinese would argue that this form of democracy is a sham since the mass of the working people are excluded from exercising effective political power. As the extract above shows, they maintain that real democracy can only be achieved by the Communist Party monopolizing political power in the interests of the working class whom the Party represents. The election of cadres at grass roots level, for example in communes and factories, and the accountability of cadres to the masses are, for the Chinese, important elements in the 'dictatorship of the proletariat'. Individual rights and the legal system are defined within this political context. This

27

chapter examines the characteristics of China's Socialist democracy. You must compare and contrast it with the British experience and judge for yourself.

THE PARTY

The ultimate aim of the Party is to bring about the realization of Communism ... [the Party] is the core of the leadership of the whole Chinese people.

Party cadres are used throughout the State administrative system to ensure Party control. For example, until 1980, Hua Guofeng was both Chairman of the Party and Premier of the State Council. Even at factory and commune level the most important positions are held by Party members; thus, cadres often have both Party and administrative duties.

The organization of the 38·5 million members of China's political élite, the Communist Party, is strictly hierarchical. As the diagram shows, at each of the four organizational levels a committee is elected by a congress of delegates from a lower level, and approved by the authorities above. These committees are charged with overseeing the work of the Party.

Constitutionally, National Party Congresses are to be held every five years, although in times of political dissent their meetings have been irregular. Since the seventh Party Congress in 1945 only four congresses have been called, the latest in 1977. The National Congress elects the Central Committee, which in turn elects the Party Chairman, the Political Bureau and its Standing Committee. Although membership of the Central Committee is a high political honour, real power lies within the Political Bureau and its Standing Committee. These are the key policy-making bodies and contain all the most important people in the Chinese leadership; meetings of both are chaired by Hua Guofeng.

The guiding principle of Party organization and communication is 'democratic centralism'. In theory, cadres at all levels, reflecting the views and opinions of the masses,

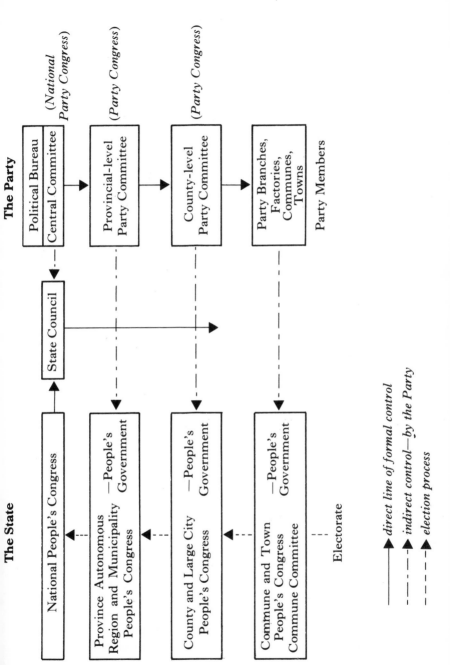

How the Party and the State are organized.

participate in the decision-making process. Once decisions are arrived at, each Party member must support and implement Party policy.

The whole Party must observe democratic centralism: the individual is subordinate to the organization, the lower level is subordinate to the higher level, and the entire Party is subordinate to the Central Committee. (Party Constitution, 1977)

THE STATE

The State system supervises the routine of government administration and implements Party policy.

The National People's Congress [N.P.C.] is the highest organ of State power ... and local People's Congresses at various levels are local organs of State power. (State Constitution, 1978)

The State structure parallels Party organization. Legislation passed in 1979 makes provision for the direct election of deputies to the congresses up to county level. Everyone over eighteen can vote and candidates from organizations other than the C.P.C. are accepted. Official encouragement is given to the nomination of more candidates than the number of deputies to be elected. Beyond county level the People's Congresses elect deputies to the next level, and so on, up to the N.P.C.

The 1978 constitution stipulates that the N.P.C shall be elected every five years, shall meet annually, and shall appoint a standing committee to conduct business in between sessions. The N.P.C. also appoints the State Council and the Premier. The latter appointment also requires the recommendation of the Central Committee of the Party. The State Council is the executive organ of the N.P.C. and at present comprises Premier Hua Guofeng, Deng Xiaoping and all 42 ministers in charge of government departments.

Although in theory the N.P.C. has very substantial powers, in that it can amend the constitution, make laws and decide on questions of war and peace, in practice it is subservient to the Party and a rubber stamp for its policies. Many of the most important policy decisions since 1949— for example, China's involvement in the Korean War, the Great Leap Forward, the Cultural Revolution, the struggle against the 'Gang of Four' and the 'Four Modernizations' —were all initiated by the Party without prior consultation with the N.P.C. In fact from 1966 to 1974 the N.P.C. did not meet at all, and the policy-making and administrative functions of the provincial and county congresses were undertaken by revolutionary committees.

As well as re-establishing the congresses and making electoral changes, the new leadership has abolished the revolutionary committees. The new organs of adminis-tration, known as People's Governments, are appointed by and are responsible to the congresses. In theory these, together with the congresses, are a means of providing political participation and accountability. This idea must be set against the fact that the Party is nevertheless accepted as policy-maker and leader. For example, a meeting of the N.P.C. in September 1980 recommended that the next National Party Congress begin a revision of the State Constitution.

THE INDIVIDUAL AND THE POLITICAL SYSTEM

Most Chinese have daily contact with Party and govern-ment officials at their place of work. Party cadres hold regular political meetings to inform people of government policy and to generate enthusiasm and activity. Mass campaigns are used to highlight specific policies. For example the present drive for the 'Four Modernizations' involves cadres in explaining the ideological significance of new pay schemes, discussing the need to increase pro-duction and urging emulation of models. Although cadres are expected to be model Communist citizens, continued press references to cases of 'back door practices' suggest that not all cadres are as committed to 'serving the people' as the leadership would like.

In spring 1980 a directive from the Central Committee stressed that cadres 'must play an exemplary role among the masses, be the first to bear hardships and the last to enjoy comforts'. It was also announced that the forthcoming twelfth National Party Congress will make provision for reform of the cadre system, including an end to the practice of being a cadre for life.

But what rights does the individual citizen have against the actions of a Party member or State employee? In the past, criticism meetings, in which cadres were expected to explain and defend their actions, and often to make self-criticisms, were frequently held. Today, apart from the campaign to criticize the 'Gang of Four', such meetings receive little publicity. Both the revised constitutions formally guarantee the right of complaint without fear of victimization, but the efficacy of such individual action is unclear.

The present leadership appears to wish to establish more formal proceedings for participation. In 1979 Chairman Hua said:

Leading cadres should be elected not only in people's communes but gradually at basic levels in factories and in mines. Elections or public opinion polls should be regularly held ... This will help promote people who are selfless and efficient and remove people who are ignorant and complacent.

So far the Chinese press has published examples of factories that have elected section chiefs, heads of workshops and shift supervisors. Party membership for such posts was not obligatory but it was stated that 'the newly elected excel in technical skill and have a high level of Socialist consciousness.'

INDIVIDUAL RIGHTS AND THE LAW

All citizens enjoy freedom of speech, correspondence, the press, assembly, association, procession and demonstration and the freedom to strike ... the right to speak out freely, air their views fully, hold great debates and write big character posters ... [They also] enjoy freedom to believe in religion and to propagate atheism. (State Constitution, 1978)

In practice the C.P.C., as protector of the Socialist system, imposes restrictions on these freedoms, suppressing what it defines as counter-revolutionary and treasonable activities. Freedom of speech, expression and demonstration are tolerated only if they do not challenge the Socialist system. For example, individuals may criticize cadres for inefficiency and for inattentiveness to the needs of the masses; they cannot question the overall authority of the Party or the appropriateness of Communism for China. This is the context in which citizens' rights are defined and practised.

The 'Hundred Flowers Campaign', initiated in 1957 by Chairman Mao, is a good illustration. Intellectuals were encouraged to air their views and to 'let a hundred flowers bloom, a hundred schools of thought contend'. Many chose to direct their attack on the Communist system; the movement was swiftly terminated. In the purge that followed, in which many intellectuals were sent for 'reform through labour', Mao made it clear that criticism must not undermine but 'consolidate all aspects of Democratic Centralism ... the Socialist path and the leadership of the Party'.

In 1976 Chairman Hua again called for a policy of 'letting a hundred flowers bloom', and although restrictions are still very evident there has been some relaxation. In 1978 and 1979 wall posters appeared on 'Democracy Wall' in Beijing expressing views that would not have been tolerated in the years after the Cultural Revolution. However, the case of Wei Jingsheng, whose poster is shown overleaf, is a good example of the limits of the new policy. After putting up his poster, Wei was arrested and, after trial, was sentenced to fifteen years' imprisonment. Though accused of giving away secrets to enemy agents and counter-revolutionaries, Wei's real crime was to hold the views he expressed in the dazibao. Since this incident in 1979, 'Democracy Wall' has been moved to a less

WEI JINGSHENG'S DAZIBAO
ON DEMOCRACY

After the defeat of the 'Gang of Four' we began to dream of democracy and prosperity again, but our odious political system has not been amended in the slightest by Hua and Deng ... the wearisome drivel of 'class struggle' has now been replaced with a new panacea—the 'Four Modernizations'.

According to Socialism, the masses hold all political power, but what rights and powers do we have for we must still obey the orders of the central authorities. If we wish to stop suffering from slavery and misery there is only one way—Democracy.

Genuine Democracy is a system which allows the people to dismiss and replace their representatives at any time and prevent them from abusing their powers. The difference between Democracy in China and in the western countries is as night and day. In our country, if in a private conversation you express the slightest doubt concerning the historical sublimity of our great helmsman Mao Zedong, you immediately see in front of you the gaping gates of a jail.

We want to become the masters of our own destiny. We need no gods and no emperors ... totalitarian Fascism can only bring us disaster; let us unite under the banner of Democracy.

As for those 'great leaders' who have swindled the people of their most precious rights for several decades, they may now all go to hell. The 'Democracy Wall' in Beijing has become the people's first fortress in the struggle against all reactionary forces whose worst examples this century are Nazi Germany, the Soviet Union and the 'New China'. Blood will be shed ... but the reactionary forces will never again succeed in obliterating our Democracy flag in their poisonous mist.

An abridged version of Wei Jingsheng's dazibao on democracy which he posted on Beijing's 'Democracy Wall'.

prominent area of Beijing and in 1980 the constitution was formally amended to exclude the 'right to hold great debates and write big character posters'.

The new legal code

Unlike most countries China has never had a written legal code. On 1 January 1980 a formal code was established. The present leadership claims that it will guarantee Socialist democracy and prevent the abuse of individual rights that allegedly occurred under the 'Gang of Four'. Its aims are to 'protect the Socialist system, maintain public order, punish criminals and protect citizens' rights and their property'. Political offences are included in the criminal code. Any act which challenges the 'dictatorship of the proletariat' is considered counter-revolutionary and therefore punishable.

Depending on the seriousness of the crime, punishment ranges from the death penalty or long prison sentences to fines and deprivation of political rights. Social pressure is an important aspect of the penal system. Trivial cases are often dealt with on a local basis. For example, neighbourhood committees hold special classes to re-educate young criminals and political deviants. Physical labour and political study often form part of the punishment.

The Chinese Economy

CHINESE AGRICULTURE

Despite the progress made since 1949, the essential task still facing the Chinese government is to increase agricultural efficiency and to raise the standard of living of the 1,000 million inhabitants of the country.

The majority of Chinese peasants, 85% of the population, live in communes which provide 99% of the total agricultural produce. The sizes of the 50 thousand communes vary and can comprise between 20,000 and 50,000 people. A commune is an economic, political and social unit, collectively owned and run by its members. It organizes agriculture and other forms of production, and provides for the social, medical and cultural welfare of its inhabitants. Communes are divided into production brigades, which in turn are sub-divided into production teams.

The obstacles to progress are formidable. Close study of the map on 'Major crops in agricultural China' shows the immense range of geographically distinct areas within China. Much of the land is unsuitable for cultivation and 90% of the population lives on 40% of the land that is called 'agricultural China'. Even within this limited area, the differences in climate and soil fertility result in a tremendous diversity in the living standards of communes.

From 1964 national attention was focused on the efforts and progress of one production brigade, located in a backward and agriculturally deprived area, Dazhai (Tachai).

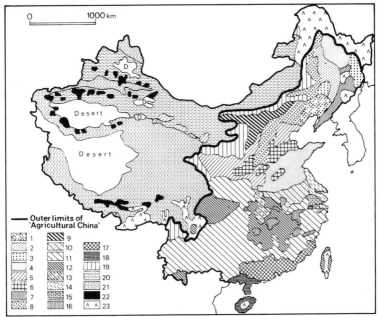

1 Cotton/Kaoliang* 2 Soybean/Kaoliang 3 Kaoliang 4 Wheat/Oil seeds
5 Wheat/Miscellaneous grains 6 Cotton/Wheat 7 Maize 8 Maize/Millet
9 Potatoes/Grain 10 Rice/Wheat 11 Rice/Maize/Timber 12 Rice
13 Cotton/Rice 14 Cotton 15 Rice/Wheat/Silk 16 Tea 17 Rice/Sugar/
Tropical fruits 18 Rubber/Tropical crops 19 Semi-farming/Livestock
20 Desert grazing 21 Mountain grazing 22 Oases of west (including
agricultural area of Xizang (Tibet)) 23 Forest   * A type of grain
The major crop areas in agricultural China.

'Learn from Dazhai'

The message of Dazhai was self-help, local initiative and
political commitment. By raising the slogan 'Learn from
Dazhai', Mao hoped to popularize both the practical and
political elements of his agricultural model.

Established in 1953 in a remote and mountainous region
of Shaanxi province, the Dazhai production brigade, which
numbered 295 people, faced severe problems. The area has
very poor topsoils and an extreme climate with alternate
periods of drought, torrential rainfall and harsh winds.
Before 1949 the inhabitants of Dazhai lived in caves and
were often on the edge of starvation. Only the landlord and
three rich peasants, who together owned two-thirds of the
land, enjoyed a secure existence.

'In agriculture learn from Dazhai,' reads the slogan in the background.

Since 1953 we have worked for years in succession without asking for state loans or free supplies to which we are entitled. Using our bare hands and carrying-poles, we have already built more than 200 mu of gully land capable of high yield, created 600 mu of ridge slope land and transformed the land into terraced fields. In 20 years our grain yield has increased from 0·75 to 7·5 tons per hectare. (Chen Yonggui, brigade leader)

As the brigade's income increased, mechanization became possible. By 1973 they owned 6 tractors, 37 trucks and 60 agricultural implements, and they had constructed 5 cable lifts to carry manure up to the highest terraces and bring quarried stone down for building projects. Production expanded to include a small noodles factory and a brickworks.

Other aspects of Dazhai life have altered equally dramatically. A local school and new houses, each with electric light and access to piped water, were built, and communal services now include a co-operative store, post office, restaurant, clinic and kindergarten.

According to Chen the success of Dazhai was entirely due to 'putting the Thoughts of Chairman Mao in command'. Political discussion and the study of Maoist texts were part of the daily routine for Dazhai peasants.

From a Maoist point of view, Dazhai was politically advanced in its egalitarian attitude towards ownership and work rates. In most communes the production team was the basic ownership level; in Dazhai, farm animals, land and implements were owned by the brigade. Mao saw as the ideal a gradual raising of the level of ownership from the team to the brigade, and ultimately to total collective ownership. Private plots and sideline activities, common practices in most communes, were abolished in Dazhai because they 'weakened the collective ideal'.

In Dazhai the brigade was also the basic accounting unit, responsible for the allocation of income amongst its members. Until 1967 most teams apportioned work points on the basis of work done and the length of time worked, heavy work being accorded more work points than light work. Points were then converted to labour days and the total distributable income divided amongst the members according to the number of labour days worked. However, in Dazhai the individual's attitude to work and his

Dazhai brigade has joined small plots together to create larger tracts of land suitable for tractor-ploughing.

commitment to the C.P.C. were also taken into account: 'We have individual assessment followed by mass discussion of the adequacy of the individual's workload and his degree of political awareness. If someone finishes work early, he goes and works elsewhere without points and "serves the people".' Material incentives and bonuses were ignored on the grounds that they 'contradicted the Socialist ideal and widened the gap between worker and worker'.

After the Cultural Revolution, the influence of Dazhai spread rapidly. National and local 'Learn from Dazhai' conferences were held and many Dazhai-type communes and brigades were formed.

Agriculture since 1976

Even before the death of Chairman Mao, the influence of Dazhai was waning. Communes in more fertile areas felt that the Dazhai approach was unsuited to their needs; that the stress on political action, the banning of sideline activities and lack of material incentives hampered production and agricultural efficiency. Another important criticism was that the emphasis on self-sufficiency and lack of direct State intervention condemned communes in less fertile areas to remain relatively poor, whilst others flourished. The present leadership specifically criticizes the nationwide attempt to 'deify' Dazhai and the mechanical implementation of the model regardless of local conditions. Significantly, Dazhai's leader, Chen Yonggui, has been removed from his post and is now undergoing political re-education.

The new leadership claims that the increase in agricultural production before 1976 was not as large as it should have been; a failure which it firmly attributes to the influence of the 'Gang of Four'. The Ten-Year Plan, issued by the new government in 1976, outlined the following objectives for agriculture:

—value of agricultural output to increase by 4–5% annually;
—400 million tonnes of grain to be produced per year by 1985;
—85% of farm activities to be mechanized by 1985;

—by 1985 farm land giving stable high yields, irrespective of droughts or water-logging, will be 1 mu per person in rural areas.

To achieve these objectives, important policy changes have been made. The agricultural tax was reduced in 1977 and 1978 to its present level of 3% in order to allow peasants to retain more of their profits, and more grants for mechanization have been made available. The importance of rural industries as a means of providing the peasants with intermediate technology and preventing the drift to the cities, continues to be stressed. In 1978 State investment in agriculture was increased from $10\cdot7\%$ to 14%, the prices of some farm products were allowed to rise and the manufacture of tractors and chemical fertilizers was given priority. Diversification is currently being encouraged in an attempt to restructure the small peasant economy, with its emphasis on grain, into a modern agricultural production system with all-round development of forestry, livestock breeding, fishing and cultivation of grain and cash crops.

At the local level the three-tier ownership of team, brigade and commune has been re-affirmed. The new State Constitution specifically mentions the team's rights and confirms its position as the basic accounting unit. It also guarantees the rights of peasants to engage in sideline activities, own a private plot, and sell their produce in local private markets known as rural fairs.

Most important of all has been the re-introduction of material incentives. Whilst lip service is paid to the role of political and moral incentives, income is now solely determined by the work each individual does: 'Only through hard work can production develop and the lives of the masses be steadily improved'. Two other recent official government statements clearly show the new direction and underline the aspects of Dazhai that are no longer to be emulated: '... political interference in production must be ended', and '...we must overcome egalitarianism and apply the principle "to each according to his work".'

However, the influence of Dazhai still persists and is officially encouraged in one important aspect. The success-

Deep ploughing

Adequate manuring

Irrigation projects

Good seed

Close planting

Plant protection

Tools reform

Field management

The Dazhai eight-point charter for agriculture.

ful implementation of the Dazhai 'Eight Point Charter' in every commune, brigade and team would do more than any other political or economic act to improve agricultural production and raise peasant living standards.

Hongqi commune

Hongqi (Red Flag) commune is, by Chinese standards, a prosperous enterprise. The main activity for its 48,000 members is to produce fresh fruit and vegetables: bananas, lychees, pineapples, cabbages and onions, which command high prices in the nearby city of Canton. Because of its favourable position, Hongqi has to grow only sufficient grain and rice for its own needs. Situated on the delta of the great river Xi Jiang, flooding in the monsoon season is a constant danger, and, wherever possible, the villages are built on high ground and protected by dykes. Through irrigation and water conservancy schemes, largely built by their own labour, the members have a plentiful supply of water. The river silt and sewage from Canton provides rich fertilizer and allows multi-cropping to take place—usually two or three crops a year.

Today the two leading bodies in Hongqi are the Party Committee and the Commune Management Committee. They have replaced the revolutionary committee established after 1968. The Party Committee is elected by the 1,470 Party members in the commune. The Commune Management Committee, which also functions as the grass roots government, is supposed to be chosen by the Commune People's Congress which is elected by the commune members. However, this system has only just been re-introduced and the democratic election of a new Management Committee has not yet been held in Hongqi. The Management Committee is composed of a chairman, who is also the secretary of the Party Committee, and thirteen members who are responsible for the work of agriculture, industry, education and culture, the Communist Youth League and the Militia. Since many of the Management Committee are also members of the Party Committee, major issues are decided by the Party Committee and implemented by the Management Committee.

Both committees work together to organize and supervise the general activities of the 33 brigades and 150 teams, working out, for example, production targets with local Party officials. Commune-owned enterprises are those too large or expensive for individual brigades to undertake. In Hongqi these are the hospital, four secondary schools, three tractor stations and a lorry repair shop.

The production brigades help the Commune Committee implement its policies and assist their own teams. The Shengli (Victory) brigade, which has 1,500 people farming 2,500 mu, is split into four teams. The brigade maintains a machine repair shop and a small brick and tile factory, and provides fertilizer. Its welfare services include a primary school, an adult literacy class and a clinic. The brigades co-operate with one another on large-scale projects, for example the building of dams, but are administratively independent and differ in wealth and income.

Comrade Xiao Wen is the leader of one of Shengli's production teams. The committee he heads is responsible for production, military, ideological and accounting affairs within the team. The total membership of the team is 350 people and there is a work force of 250, one third of whom are under sixteen years of age. The members work long hours in the growing season and attend to private business and capital construction projects in the slack months between November and February. Although private plots and sideline activities are now officially encouraged, work on these has to be done outside normal working hours.

Responsible for its own gains and losses, the production team organizes agricultural and sideline activities, handles matters of daily life for commune members and decides on the distribution of income. As the basic accounting unit, Xiao's team must decide the number of work points to be allocated to the various tasks. Each year the team divides its total income; the State tax must be paid, quotas fulfilled, and sums set aside for the public welfare and accumulation funds, before the members can receive their share. These two funds provide for education and welfare services and for investment in farm machinery and other equipment. Last year they were allocated respectively 8% and 9% of

Members of Juyi commune, Henan, harvest rice.

the team's income. As the production team is a small-scale organization, in larger matters such as production plans, construction projects and industrial management the team is subordinate to the brigade and commune.

Like all the other peasants in the village, Xiao and his wife own their house, which they bought with their savings. With their two sons they live in a small whitewashed building comprising a living-room, bedroom, small kitchen and outside toilet. The rooms are sparsely furnished with two beds, a table, several chairs and some large jars for storing rice. Clothes are made at home from cotton provided by the team. As well as a sewing-machine, the family owns a radio, two bicycles and an electric clock.

As in most communes, pay at Hongqi is partially 'in kind'. Last year the Xiao family received 2 jin of raw cotton, 450 jin of grain, 17½ feet of cotton cloth, and various foodstuffs such as meat, vegetables, cooking-oil and some fuel. The total cash value of this was 100 yuan and, in addition, Xiao earned 480 yuan and his wife 230 yuan. Living expenses are low; the fuel they use comes from leftovers such as corn husks, and their private plot provides extra income and vegetables. The Xiaos are able to save approximately 25% of their income, but consumer goods are still in short supply and very expensive.

45

Outside working hours the family are involved in militia training, evening classes and political meetings, though the latter are less frequent and intense than in recent years. Their proximity to Canton enables Hongqi members to have greater opportunities for entertainment and affords them access to medical and educational facilities. Most communes are less privileged; they are reliant on their own local welfare services and the occasional visits of travelling film shows and theatre groups.

INDUSTRY

'Agriculture the foundation, industry the leading factor'

The cornerstone of Maoist economic policy was to establish the correct balance between agriculture and industry. As we have seen, his spiral of development was firmly based on an expanding rural economy, which he believed would ultimately provide the funds for industrial expansion. Whilst the model did not minimize the importance of industrial investment, the priority was to improve agricultural productivity, and to ensure this industry was required, where possible, to support the rural sector. Mao's strategy was usually referred to as 'Agriculture the foundation, industry the leading factor'.

'Without agriculture there can be no light industry.'

After 1968 a whole range of small-scale light industries was established, producing, for example, agricultural machinery and tools, textiles, electrical goods and bicycles. The relationship between the two economic sectors was reciprocal; light industry would utilize agricultural raw materials, such as cotton, jute, and wool, and in turn provide the rural sector with consumer goods and the machinery required to boost agriculture. In 1973, for example, national praise was lavished on a small engineering plant in Harbin which produced midget water turbine generators. These could be used by communes to produce electricity for lighting, rice threshing and wheat milling. They were of particular use in mountainous areas; '... gone is the time when rivers flowed by down below while water was as expensive as cooking-oil up on the hills.'

Where possible, light industries were established in rural areas. Communes were encouraged to set up small factories which would supply their own needs and use local resources. It was hoped that these industries would soak up rural unemployment resulting from increased agricultural mechanization.

'As agriculture and light industry develop, heavy industry, assured of its funds and markets, will grow faster.'

Under Mao, State investment in the major heavy industries such as coal-mining, machine-building, steel, petroleum and chemicals continued to be substantial; however, the emphasis was on gearing heavy industry to agricultural needs. For example, in the period 1965–75 the output of electric generators, machine tools, internal combustion engines, tractors, automobile and locomotive equipment was estimated to have increased more than three times. In order to promote local development and halt the growth of urban areas within the Eastern coastal regions, new heavy industrial projects were located in the provinces. Reports suggest that by 1974 each county had its own plants producing iron, chemical fertilizer and farm machinery.

An important consequence of these policies and the emphasis placed on locally-initiated development was the decline of national planning. Decision-making was referred to the provincial and lower levels.

Mao's political objective was the elimination of the 'three great differences'; differences between town and country, worker and peasant, and mental and manual labour. To counter the growing differentials between the urban and rural sectors, industrial workers' wages were held static by the introduction of the 8-point wage scale, which ranged from 36–108 yuan a month. Bonuses and incentive wage schemes were officially discouraged because they increased differentials and weakened co-operative ideals. After 1968 the organization and running of factories was the re-sponsibility of the revolutionary committee, which contained representatives from the workers. In order to ensure their contact with the workers and to guard against 'bureaucratic practices', all managers and cadres were obliged to undertake regular periods of work on the shop floor.

'Learn from Daqing'

Combine town with country, industry with agriculture, in industry learn from Daqing.

The Daqing (Taching) oilfield, situated in Heilongjiang, China's most northerly province, was from 1968 publicized as an industrial model. For the tens of thousands of workers and demobilized P.L.A. soldiers who were despatched to Daqing in 1960, living and working conditions were extremely hard. In temperatures as low as $-30°$ Fahrenheit, the workers and their families lived in tents on the snow-bound grasslands whilst oil drilling began and homes were constructed. However, progress was rapid. It is claimed that from 1960 the output of crude oil increased by 28% annually and that the funds accumulated are at present 14·5 times the total State investment in Daqing.

But Daqing was most famous for the way it combined agriculture with industry. Surrounding the drilling and processing installations, farming areas were established, tended by the oil workers and their families, and instead of a large city, 60 worker-peasant villages were built, each housing 5,000 people. The villages form independent communities and aim to be self-sufficient in food. In 1978 Daqing produced 410,000 tonnes of grain, 1·45 million tonnes of vegetables and 8,400 tonnes of edible oil.

Daqing embodied the Maoist principles of hard work, self-sufficiency and political commitment. Individuals like 'Iron man Wang Qiuxi' became national labour heroes, famous for their dedication to increased production. It was also one of the first large enterprises to institute Mao's principles for industrial management, known as the 'Anshan Constitution', introducing cadre participation in labour, and worker participation in management. At the time of the Cultural Revolution, Daqing was quick to establish revolutionary committees and involve their managers and workers in political study.

The achievements of Daqing were, for Mao, both politically correct and economically impressive. The much-needed oil was produced, and food and employment were found for the workers and their families, thus reducing the burden on the State and blurring the distinction between town and country. In Maoist terminology, urban and rural activities were mutually supportive, not antagonistic.

INDUSTRY SINCE 1976

The present leadership's stated aim of making China a modern, industrial country has resulted in some dramatic changes in industrial policy. The official view, however, is that agriculture is still the 'foundation of the economy'. Statements in 1979 and 1980 continued to emphasize the importance of rural industries, both as a major contributor to the economy and as a means of raising peasants' living standards. The government also stresses the number of new

Bulldozers ready to leave the Shanghai Pengpu Machinery Plant. Workers and cadres of the plant have ushered in a new upsurge in the 'Learn from Daqing' movement, thanks to their deepening criticism of the crimes of the 'Gang of Four'.

industrial projects, for instance in the production of tractors and chemical fertilizers, which are designed to aid agriculture. Daqing still receives official support. It is now viewed as an appropriate strategy for some, but not all, of China's enterprises. No doubt this is not just because the model is relevant to China's economic situation, but also because of the political significance of Daqing as one of the industrial centres where, according to all accounts, the 'Gang of Four' failed to find support.

The new leadership presents its industrial innovations as counter-measures to the anarchy caused by the Gang. They claim that under the Gang, 24% of all industries ran at a loss and there was a substantial decline in productivity. According to one factory manager the Gang 'set national self-reliance against learning what is advanced from other countries. The situation was chaotic, workers turned up late and went home early. Affairs were run by a revolutionary committee which was not interested in skills or organization.'

In the Ten-Year Plan issued in 1976, Chairman Hua outlined the short-term industrial objectives:
— an annual increase in industrial production of 10%;
— one third of enterprises to be Daqing-type;
— 120 major new projects;
— automation of major industrial processes;
— build-up of heavy industry.

A most important development has been the willingness of the present government to undertake huge foreign loans to purchase western technology. From 1972 China began to extend her foreign trade, but the size of the present agreements, in particular those with the U.S.A., Japan and the E.E.C., is quite unprecedented. Extreme national self-sufficiency has clearly ended. Chinese managers and experts are now being urged to 'learn from the advanced science, technology and managerial expertise of the developed capitalist countries, to speed up the "Four Modernizations".'

According to Chairman Hua the economy will 'proceed by planned proportionate development'. In order to increase industrial efficiency and productivity, strict planning schemes and new production targets have been introduced. Revolutionary committees no longer exist. The Party Committee is responsible for ensuring that targets are fulfilled and that central directives are implemented. The day-to-day administration of factories is now left to the managers and experts, who have regained much of their old status. Cadre participation in labour and political study, although officially supported, now receives less attention.

Under Mao, self-sufficiency led to the development of groups of industries which would serve a local area. This is now regarded as wasteful of resources and causing unnecessary duplication. Instead, specialization is encouraged; each new project will produce goods for a much larger area. Profitability and industrial efficiency are the criteria which all enterprises must meet.

One of the first actions of the new leaders was to raise industrial wages. Incentive wage schemes and bonus payments now receive positive encouragement and are justified by the principle 'to each according to his work'.

> In the cause of Socialist construction it is permissible that in some areas and enterprises workers will get more pay because they have made greater efforts. This will encourage others to learn from them and bring about a steady development in the national economy ... Eliminating the differences may sound very nice but it is ridiculous if no efforts are made to develop production. Empty talk will only tarnish the banner of Socialism and plunge society into chaos. (*People's Daily*, 1978)

1980

By 1980 it was clear that the economic improvement hoped for by the new leadership was not materializing:

> In 1976 the national economy was on the verge of collapse. From 1976 to 1979 we overcame a multitude of difficulties but we incurred a number of grave losses in economic construction ... The targets of the Ten-Year Plan were too high and we overstressed heavy industry at the expense of agriculture and light industry ... (Chairman Hua, September 1980)

In the course of the year, further changes in economic policy were announced, most of which bear the mark of the newly-promoted Zhao Ziyang. A new Ten-Year Plan is being prepared for the period 1981–90; its targets will be more realistic and it will direct State investment from the heavy industrial sector to agriculture and light industry. Owing to the lack of foreign exchange, drastic cuts have been made in the schemes to import foreign technology. Consistent with Zhao's pragmatic approach, increased production is the sole aim. State interference in economic activity will be further reduced, competition between economic units encouraged, and a flourishing private economy in the town and the countryside is expected and officially applauded. For instance, communes are to maximize output according to local conditions; individual enterprises and co-operative profit-making ventures between communes and factories are praised. Premier Zhao has said that the decision-making powers of factory managers must be 'vigorously expanded'. Within the overall framework of the Socialist plan, plants and factories are to compete with one another for markets on the basis of supply and demand.

As part of the rationalization, the State has stopped subsidizing wasteful and inefficient plants, and local industries are directed to borrow from the bank and not to ask for State aid. For the first time for many years the Bank of China has begun advancing loans to private businesses. By mid-1980 more than 300,000 licences had been issued to the 'self-employed', that is, individuals, husband-and-wife teams or syndicates of profit-sharing partners who make furniture, repair watches or run a variety of enterprises ranging from barber's shops to laundries. Perhaps even more interesting is the Manchurian factory praised for its efforts to raise capital by selling shares to its workers. In Sichuan, the Province for which Zhao was formerly responsible, the joint stock companies set up in the mid-70s on an experimental basis are now held up as models for the whole of China.

For 'China watchers' the rate of change in economic policy is surprising; for Maoists the changes are ominous.

Only as the situation develops in the 1980s will we be able to evaluate the extent to which the Maoist economic model still has relevance in China.

Taiyuan

One of the biggest factories in the city of Taiyuan in Shanxi Province is the iron and steel works which employs 15,000 people. Whilst some workers live in houses in different parts of the city, the majority stay with their families in the neighbourhood complex surrounding the factory which is called Douzheng ('Struggle').

Within Douzheng a number of social and recreational facilities are provided. For example, the neighbourhood's 20,000 children are taught in 7 middle, 14 primary and 13 nursery schools. The neighbourhood also has a number of small factories and service industries which provide part-time and temporary employment, e.g. textile workshops, a bicycle repair works, restaurants and laundries.

The iron and steel works

Responsibility for the Taiyuan works lies with the factory directors, under the leadership of the works Party Committee. Elected by the Party members in the works, the Party Committee meets once a month to take important decisions affecting production. It is its job to see that national policy is implemented at the works level. The Political Department, an administrative body of the Party Committee, organizes propaganda, militia and trade-union affairs. The Works Director and his deputies look after the day-to-day running of the enterprise and are responsible for production, planning, technology and research, safety, product quality and wages. The Workers' Congresses, elected by the workers in Taiyuan, voice workers' opinions and channel demands and requests to the leadership. They take part in discussions on major issues, put forward criticisms and proposals for improving production, and supervise the leading cadres. On the shop floor, shift and group leaders are democratically elected by the workers.

The Taiyuan works operates a system of three shifts of eight hours each, and an eight-grade wage scale ranging

Inside a general store.

from 42 to 108 yuan a month. The policy 'to each according to his work' is followed. Smelting-room workers receive 20 yuan a month more than those doing auxiliary jobs. The highest production bonus a steel worker can earn amounts to 22.5% of his standard wage. In 1978 the average annual wage for a furnace face-worker was 780 yuan.

The factory dominates the lives of its workers; it is much more than a place of employment. It provides medical care, organizes political study and social and recreational activities, and issues work cards, ration coupons, travel permits and even library tickets.

Fang Honglin and his wife Su Yingchao both work in the factory. In 1980 Fang earned 680 yuan and Su 504 yuan. Although these wages seem low, they pay no income tax, receive free medical treatment and pay only half of the medical expenses of their two sons. On retirement both will be entitled to a pension equivalent to 80% of their salary. Living costs, for example rent, fares, electricity and food, are also relatively low.

Nearly all the family's daily needs are served by their general store and local clinic. There is also an open market which Su visits frequently. All prices are subject to government control, and goods such as grain and cotton, which are in short supply, are rationed. Although the neighbourhood provides a fairly big store, a post office and a bank, Su occasionally catches a bus into town to visit friends and to do her shopping in the larger stores.

The family rent their flat from the factory for 8 yuan a month. It has two rooms but no running water; they share a kitchen and a toilet with four other families who live on the same floor. During the week the family often eat in the factory canteen. Within the household nothing is wasted; bottles and plastic bags are saved and re-used and little importance is attached to having new clothes if old ones can be mended.

Each year the family save about 20% of their total income towards the cost of household goods, which are both expensive and in short supply. They already own two bicycles, a sewing-machine, a radio and two wrist-watches and would like to purchase a camera.

Within their own residential area the Fangs mix freely with their neighbours. In the warm weather they often eat and relax in the street with their friends. Because of the shortage of formal leisure and entertainment facilities, recreational activities are mostly , self-organized. On Sundays and national holidays, such as May Day and National Day (1 October) the family like to go out. They might visit the local park or cinema, or go into Taiyuan to the museum or zoo.

Sports, especially table tennis and basketball, are very popular and each morning Fang joins the many other workers who go to the park to practise the art of shadow-boxing.

Aspects of Chinese Society

EDUCATION UNDER MAO

All Communists see education as vital to Socialist development. They regard education as reflecting the economic system of a country and its dominant class. Despite the advance made between 1949 and 1966, Mao criticized the educational system for perpetuating the élitist and bourgeois ideas of the 'old' society. The changes instigated after 1968, Mao believed, would ensure the continuation of the class struggle and the future of Socialist development.

> Our education policy must enable everyone ... to develop morally, intellectually, and physically and become a worker with Socialist consciousness. (Mao Zedong, 1957)

> Whilst their main task is to study, they should also learn other things, that is, industrial work, farming and military affairs. They should also criticize the bourgeoisie. (Mao Zedong directive, 7 May 1966)

After the Cultural Revolution much more time was spent on political discussion and the study of Communist writers such as Marx, Lenin and Mao Zedong. As the excerpts from the school textbooks show, political study was not confined to specific periods on the timetable. Chinese language lessons often involved the study of Mao's works, and mathematics lessons meant the calculation of problems concerning agricultural or industrial production. The themes of 'hating pre-Communist society', 'being a good

The Party
I have often felt that the party is my mother. If it weren't for the Party where would today's happiness be? I must study hard, forever going with the Party.

Yesterday and Today
Grandpa at seven went begging,
Papa at seven fled famine,
This year I am also seven,
And happily I go to school.

Studying and Labouring
We love to study,
We love to labour,
We labour, we study,
We study, we labour.
We study hard at learning skills,
We are diligent from the time we are little.
Having learned skills, we go out to plant the fields.
Having learned skills, we go out to do work.

Excerpts from Chinese language textbooks still used in primary schools.

8.00	School opens Assembly: political lesson is read
8.10	Six fifty-minute periods with breaks mid-morning and lunchtime
15.40	Current affairs discussion group
16.00	Extra curricular activities
18.30	School closes

Syllabus

Political study	Basic agricultural knowledge
Chinese	Physical training
English	Art and hygiene
Maths	Physics
Chemistry	

The timetable and syllabus of an average middle school.

Socialist', 'taking part in production' and 'serving the people and the Party' were ever present, and it must be remembered that many of these textbooks are still in use today.

> Education must serve proletarian politics and be combined with productive labour. (Mao Zedong, 1966)

After 1966 renewed emphasis was placed on participation in manual labour by all pupils, students and teachers. Although this benefited the economy, its primary purpose was political. Mao believed that manual work would remove the feelings of arrogance and superiority that educated people often displayed towards the peasants and workers. All school timetables included work in a local commune, school workshop or allotment, and university teachers and their students were expected to spend their vacations helping out in the countryside.

In schools and universities the traditional highly-competitive exams were abolished. The new entrance qualifications for the much-sought-after university places required middle-school graduates to have worked for two years in a commune or factory, to possess an immaculate

An illustration from a primary school textbook.

political record and a recommendation from their fellow-workers. Less stress was placed on academic excellence, and some universities accepted a quota of workers and peasants regardless of their qualifications.

> This old examination system ... is most harmful to our Socialist cause. It places not proletarian politics but bourgeois politics in command ... It shuts out many outstanding children of workers, poor and lower-middle peasants ... and opens the gates wide to the bourgeoisie to cultivate its own successors. (*People's Daily*, 1968)

The previously high status of the teacher diminished under the new system. Pupils were encouraged to continue the criticism of teachers to ensure their correct political attitude.

EDUCATION SINCE 1976

In many respects the system outlined still exists but the present leadership's new priorities have resulted in some important changes.

> We must train workers with high attainment in science and culture ... if we are to master modern science ... if we are to create higher productivity than under Capitalism and transform China into a powerful modern Socialist country, and, what is more, ultimately defeat the bourgeoisie. These demands are in the interests of proletarian politics. (Deng Xiaoping, 1978)

For the new leaders, high academic standards are all-important. They claim standards fell in the previous ten years as a result of the over-concentration on politics and manual labour and the lack of competitive exams. The faults of the post-Cultural Revolution system they attribute to the 'Gang of Four', who are criticized for having led the educational revolution astray and for their anti-intellectual attitude. It is said that they labelled all teachers as bourgeois and fermented student rebellion and indiscipline.

The major educational objective of the new leaders is to create sufficient numbers of highly-qualified experts to carry out the 'Four Modernizations'. Mao's famous directive of 7 May 1966 is being re-interpreted. 'Study first' now receives much attention. Examinations have been re-introduced in schools and universities. Prospective university students must show evidence of high academic ability and a good political attitude, and the two-year period of work service is no longer compulsory.

A number of 'key' schools have appeared where outstanding pupils are sent for specialist education. It is currently being argued that 'selecting the best and training them to be experts is not necessarily linked with the formation of privileged strata.'

Participation in manual labour for pupils and students is at present under debate, and evidence is coming to light which suggests that political study is now less important. Recent directives to those engaged in scientific work, for example, state that five-sixths of their time must be spent on their subject-matter.

Educational provision is not uniform in China. Many rural areas have only the schools and colleges that limited commune funds can provide, and these are often run on a part-time basis. Some children only receive primary schooling sufficient to make them literate (acquisition of 2,500 characters) and numerate. Plans announced in 1978 set 1985 as the target year for making senior middle school (to age seventeen) universal in cities, and junior middle school (to age fourteen or fifteen) in rural areas. Efforts will also be made to enrol pupils at six instead of seven years of age.

To create the necessary number of experts in medicine, engineering and science, the proportion of the national budget devoted to science and education has been increased and a State Planning Commission for all scientific and technical work has been created. New textbooks are planned to provide up-to-date scientific information, although it is likely that, in the first instance, these will only be for the few 'key' schools and universities.

We must raise the political and social status of the people's teachers. (Deng Xiaoping, 1980)

The campaign to criticize the 'bourgeois intellectuals' has ended; the new leaders appear to be more concerned to grant teachers renewed respèct. It is claimed that the efforts to 're-educate' intellectuals have been largely successful and what is more important is to use these people to further China's education programme. In universities the professional grades of assistant, lecturer and professor have been restored and material incentives are now used to encourage people to dedicate their lives to teaching. The model teacher is now someone who favours academic attainment and keeps good discipline in the classroom.

The changes that have been described are undoubtedly not the end of the story. Educational policy clearly reflects the changing attitudes and priorities of the Chinese leadership. One theme remains constant; the central role that education plays in supporting the current Party line.

CULTURE

> There is no such thing as art ... that is detached from politics ... As Lenin said, 'Literature and art should serve the ... tens of millions of working people.' (Mao Zedong, talking at the Yanan Forum on Art and Literature, 1942)

The belief that 'culture should serve Socialism' justifies the Party's control of all cultural activities. But what 'serves Socialism' is itself subject to interpretation and so at different times the Party leadership has imposed varying degrees of control.

During the Cultural Revolution artists and writers were severely restricted. All western and foreign influences and many classical and modern Chinese art forms were suppressed. Instead, the Chinese people were offered a diet of strictly proletarian culture, the best example of which was the revolutionary opera, a combination of mime, ballet, music and drama. In *The Red Lantern*, set in the anti-Japanese war, the hero, a railway worker and Party member, suffers torture and dies rather than reveal the message he is trying to convey to the Red guerrillas in the nearby mountains. The political message is stark; love for the Communist cause overrides personal love and necessitates individual sacrifice.

Culture today

Relatively speaking, the attitude of the present leadership is more permissive. Foreign books and plays have been re-published, western-style music and ballet are again permitted and orchestras and music schools are being re-established. However, cultural activities are still tightly controlled.

> Writers and artists should ... portray pioneers in the modernization drive ... should give the people both education and entertainment ... and should carry out a protracted struggle against ideas that obstruct the 'Four Modernizations'. (Deng Xiaoping, 1979)

The new plays which receive public acclaim are those that reflect current ideological thinking. *Yang Kuimai*, for instance, was praised for depicting Mao 'not as he was deified by the Gang, but as a vigorous and great leader'. *The Call of the Future* deals with the difference in attitude between factory cadres. One sticks rigidly to 'authoritative works' and refuses expert advice, the other, the hero, uses his initiative to 'blaze a new trail and adopt new measures for modernization'.

HEALTH

Life expectancy in China before 1949 was short. The causes of death were typical of those of a Third World country—starvation, malnutrition, infectious and parasitic diseases. Some estimates suggest that an average of 4 million people, half the annual death toll, died from diseases readily preventable by modern public health methods. To serve a population approaching 550 million there were approximately 12,000 qualified doctors. Most hospitals and doctors were located in the cities and were for the rich only; for the majority of the population, especially in the rural areas, medical care simply did not exist.

Today the situation is radically different. Although national statistics on the state of health in China are not available, a number of studies by western experts, from which estimates can be made, suggest enormous achievements. For example, the estimates are that between 1949 and 1973 the infant mortality rate dropped from approximately 200 per 1,000 live births to a national figure of 28 per 1,000 (12–15 per 1,000 in some cities). Other studies show that in some areas the leading causes of death, as in western countries, are now cancer and heart disease. Most visitors to China note the apparent health of the population in contrast to other under-developed countries, and comment on the general cleanliness of the environment and the constant attention paid to health care.

The substantial rise in living standards achieved since 1949 has done much to improve the nation's health. With only 8% of the world's cultivable land, China presently feeds one-quarter of the world's population. Agricultural progress and a more equal distribution of food resources have provided an adequate, albeit nutritionally basic, diet for all Chinese. However, equally important has been the spread of health-care facilities. In constructing a health service the Chinese have focused on public health, preventive medicine, the training of a variety of medical personnel and the use of traditional as well as western medical techniques. With the pressure on national resources the emphasis has been on providing a basic level of care rather than specialist treatment, and on serving the needs of the rural communities. The concept of the 'barefoot doctor' underlies China's approach to health care.

During the 1950s large numbers of doctors were trained—an estimated 48,500 by 1959— but it was evident that health-care facilities were still largely concentrated in the urban areas. During the Great Leap Forward the training of 'barefoot doctors' to serve in rural areas began, a trend which increased after the Cultural Revolution. Today there are approximately 1·8 million 'barefoot doctors', one for every 500 of the population. Their training is a three to six months' course at the county or commune hospital and annual secondment for refresher courses. Instruction is given in basic anatomy, physiology, elementary surgery, the diagnosis and treatment of common ailments and diseases, and traditional medicine. As members of a production team, 'barefoot doctors' divide their time between farm work and medical duties. They are the first line of defence in medical care, responsible for basic treatment, vaccination, check-ups, information and education about family planning and some kinds of mass screening. They refer more complex cases to their better-qualified colleagues in the brigade health station or commune hospital.

To qualify as a fully-trained doctor takes five years' study. In order to increase the number of medical workers more rapidly, China also trains 'middle-grade' doctors who undertake a three-year course. The best of the 'barefoot doctors' are encouraged to enter the 'middle-grade' colleges in order to increase their expertise. Currently the Chinese claim to have a total of $2\frac{1}{2}$ million professional health workers.

An important feature of the Chinese system is the stress placed on preventive medicine. By instituting mass vaccination and education about public health, diseases such as smallpox, typhus, cholera, tuberculosis and schistosomiasis, which previously claimed the lives of millions annually, have now been almost totally eradicated. All health workers participate fully in public health campaigns, stressing the need for pest control, clean water supplies, adequate sanitation and personal hygiene.

Traditional medicine has long been practised in China; the first records date from the year 400 B.C. Since the Cultural Revolution the Chinese have sought to develop these techniques, particularly the use of herbal medicine and acupuncture. Most communes grow their own herbs to supply local dispensaries.

Acupuncture is the insertion of fine needles into various parts of the body to treat chronic illnesses such as arthritis and rheumatism. A modern application of acupuncture has been as an alternative to anaesthetics. It is used for a variety of operations including major abdominal surgery and open-heart surgery. The patient remains conscious throughout and is therefore able to co-operate with the surgeon. It is

A woodcut showing 'barefoot doctors' at work in a commune.

Surgeons perform an open-heart operation with a heart-lung machine, under acupuncture anaesthesia. The patient, a young girl, is fully conscious and aware of every step in the operation, but feels no pain.

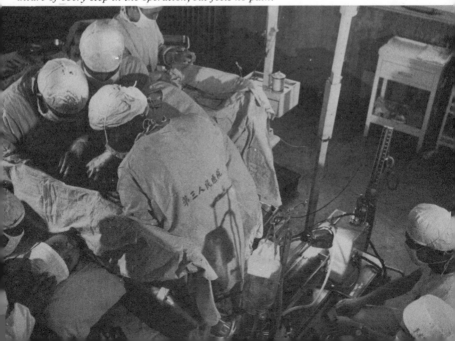

also claimed that the patient recovers faster as there are no side-effects from the use of drugs. Both acupuncture and herbal treatments have the advantage of being cheap and readily available in poorly-equipped rural clinics. The Chinese view traditional medicine not as an alternative, but as an important supplement to western techniques, given the shortage of national resources. However, Chinese medicine also claims some scientific breakthroughs. Progress in the treatment of burns and in the rejoining of severed limbs has received worldwide recognition.

Despite the efforts of the last few years there is still considerable variation in the provision of health care. Commune hospitals, although adequate, do not have the equipment, staff or specialist care that is available in the city hospitals. As communes have been largely responsible for setting up their own co-operative health schemes, the quality of care depends on the prosperity of the commune itself.

Population policy

Launch a vigorous movement for family planning and reduce the population growth rate to below 1%. (Slogan issued in 1979)

An important result of the improvement in living standards and the availability of health care has been the rapid growth in China's population, from 540 million in 1949 to a currently-estimated 1,000 million. However, it is only since the Cultural Revolution that the government has positively encouraged a policy of controlled population growth, and with some success. The Chinese claim that the average growth rate per 1,000 population has dropped from 23·4 in 1971 to 12 in 1978. This has been achieved by promoting family planning through education and by making a full range of contraceptives freely available throughout China. Social pressure has also been a major factor favouring late marriage, at age twenty-five for women and twenty-eight for men, and two children per family.

The new government has stated that greater increases in living standards can only be achieved if population growth is limited even further. As one Chinese demographer said recently, '... if we had paid attention to the control of population growth at the beginning of the '50s ... we would now be leading a much better life'.

In 1979 the government announced new targets for population growth: 5 per 1,000 by the year 1985 and a zero growth rate by the year 2,000. The methods to be employed to achieve these targets are at present under discussion, and the experience of Sichuan, China's most populous province which has recently reduced its annual growth rate to 6·06 per 1,000, is being given national publicity. The stress is on education and the cultivation of the 'correct' ideological viewpoint. By this the Chinese mean general acceptance of the idea that one child per family will be in the national interest. It is suggested that in urban areas couples with only one child will be given a health subsidy and priority in employment and housing. In rural areas the one-child family may receive extra work points, grain rations and priority in housing and the distribution of land for private plots. It is also recognized that greater provision will have to be made for the old who are without children to help them.

WOMEN IN CHINA

'Women hold up half of heaven,' said Mao Zedong. Article 53 of China's constitution confirms the equal status of men and women in political, economic and social life. The position of women has fundamentally altered in the years of Communist rule. Before 1949, women were the most degraded section of society, lacking rights in law and by custom. A woman's main duty was to produce male children to perpetuate the family line; the birth of a daughter often meant that the husband took a second wife. The sale of wives and daughters was commonplace and female babies were sometimes killed at birth. Marriages were arranged by the head of the family and women had no say in the choice of husband, and no rights to divorce, or to inherit wealth or property. Subject in turn to the authority of their fathers, their husbands, and (as widows) their sons, women endured a slave-like existence. A traditional saying was 'Noodles are not rice and women are not human beings. A wife married is like a pony bought.'

The Marriage Law of 1950 established a basis for women's equality. It abolished feudal marriage and instituted 'the new democratic marriage system ... based on free choice of partners, on monogamy, on equal rights for both sexes and on the protection of the lawful interests of women and children.' (Article 1) 'Bigamy, concubinage, child betrothal, interference in the re-marriage of widows and the extraction of gifts in connection with marriages [are] prohibited.' (Article 2) The law also established the rights of both partners to hold property, to seek work, to engage in social activity and to divorce. Care of children was fixed as the duty of both parents.

However, it was also recognized that legal changes alone are insufficient. In line with Marx and Lenin, the Chinese see participation in the economy as a prerequisite for

Women electricians.

women's emancipation. Although in some parts of China women had always worked outside the home, this was through necessity rather than as a measure of their liberation. In 1949 Mao called on all women to 'unite and participate in productive labour to improve their political and economic status'. The Great Leap Forward provided the impetus; large numbers of women took their place alongside men in the fields and factories. Today a majority of women work, many of them in jobs traditionally reserved for men, such as engineering, bus and train driving, and building work. Women workers are entitled to paid maternity leave of 56 days, pre- and post-natal care, and time off to feed their infant when they return to work. Most factories provide crêches and kindergartens, and many neighbourhoods and communes provide their own child-minding services. The availability of contraceptives and the trend towards smaller families have also been important factors in liberating women.

Through its committees, established in every village and neighbourhood, the All China Democratic Women's Federation continues to promote and protect women's rights and highlight obstacles to equality. The provision of child-minding services in some rural areas is poor. Very often it is the grannies who are still expected to look after the children. Equal pay for equal work is the rule, but there are plenty of complaints from women that their skills go unrecognized and that they are assigned work below their capabilities. There is a particular problem in communes where heavy work is assigned more work points than light work. It is hoped that increased mechanization will eventually diminish the importance of sheer physical strength. Politically women are still very under-represented. Only 14 out of 201 members of the Central Committee are women.

China's View of the World

Until the nineteenth century China regarded herself as the 'centre of the world'. Isolated from the rest of the world, she was surrounded by tributary states who recognized Chinese suzerainty by paying annual tribute to Beijing. By 1900 China had not only lost her influence over neighbouring countries but was herself the subject of colonial exploitation. The hatred of foreign domination bred a strong sense of nationalism in Chinese of all political persuasions. Indeed it was the C.P.C.'s firm nationalist stand in the war against Japan that led many to support the Communist cause. These historical factors have had an important bearing on Chinese thinking about foreign policy, which since 1949 has had two main purposes: the desire not to be dominated or humiliated by any other foreign power, and an obsessive concern with the security of China's borders. Although these considerations have remained constant, the partners with whom China has allied herself in the interests of her own security have changed. In the 1950s, whilst America sought to 'contain' Communism, China turned to the Soviet Union for internal and international support. However, with the deterioration in Sino-Soviet relations during the 1960s, China found herself in isolation, a situation which ended in the early 1970s with the beginning of Sino-American friendship.

Today China's foreign policy is conducted in accordance with the 'Three Worlds Theory', first elucidated by Mao in 1973. This theory describes the power relationships between the different countries in the world:

The Soviet Union and the United States form the first world—they are the biggest oppressors and exploiters in the world today. It is in these two countries that a new world war will inevitably break out ... they have been carrying out a furious arms race ... both work to control and subvert other countries. The second world comprises the developed countries in Europe, Japan and Canada. They are characterized by a tendency to exploit the Third World nations ... on the other hand they also suffer from superpower oppression. The third world comprises all the other hundred-odd nations in Asia, Africa and South America—although politically independent they all still face the historic task of struggling against imperialism and the new and old forms of colonialism ... (Huang Hua, Chinese Foreign Minister, 1979)

CHINA AND THE FIRST WORLD
Sino-Soviet relations
The origins of the Sino-Soviet dispute are both ideological and territorial. In 1950 the Chinese accepted Russian leadership and assistance and the two countries were firmly tied in the 'Treaty of Friendship, Alliance and Mutual Aid'. Whilst Stalin ruled, relations remained stable, but when Khrushchev came to power the dispute began to develop.

As we have already seen in Chapter 2, Mao was critical of the Soviet model as it was implemented in China. But he also pointed to a privileged class of bureaucrats and skilled personnel in Russia and saw Khrushchev's attempts to boost their living standards as further evidence that the revolutionary cause had been abandoned and that Russia was attempting to emulate the Capitalist West. Mao's attitude and personal views on development were a challenge to the Soviet position as chief interpreter of Marxist doctrine. He also questioned Russia's right to determine foreign policy for all Communist countries.

In 1956 serious differences emerged. At the twentieth Congress of the C.P.S.U. Khrushchev, in a secret speech, denounced Stalin, advocated peaceful co-existence with the West and suggested that European Communist parties could win political power through the ballot-box rather than by revolution. In Mao's eyes Khrushchev's proposals were revisionist in that they rejected the idea of the international Communist movement. Mao argued instead that the Communist nations should adopt a more militant attitude towards the West.

Correspondingly, the Russian attitude towards China hardened and the promise to give China the atomic bomb was not honoured. The Soviet press denounced the Great Leap Forward as a dangerous experiment and in 1960 all the advisers and aid given previously to China by the Russians were withdrawn.

Throughout the sixties, polemics between the two countries continued, each accusing the other of revisionism. However, the Soviet invasion of Czechoslovakia in 1968 was undoubtedly a shock to the Chinese. The *People's Daily* criticized 'those who are Socialist in words and Imperialist in deeds'. The Chinese had long felt that the Soviets were unsympathetic to Chinese security problems, and had been disappointed by the lack of support from Russia in their disputes with Taiwan and India. The Chinese now became increasingly suspicious of Soviet intentions.

In 1969 and 1970 actual conflict took place between Russian and Chinese troops over disputed territory in the River Amur area on the Sino-Soviet border. Fearing an invasion, China strengthened her forces along the border but by 1972 the Soviet Union had 10,000 tanks, 25% of her combat aircraft and 1 million troops facing the P.L.A. Mao advised preparation for a protracted people's war: 'Dig tunnels deep, store grain everywhere, accept no hegemony.'

'Hegemony' now became the code word used by the Chinese to describe the 'expansionist' desires of the Soviet Union, a view which the new Chinese leadership has maintained, despite recent attempts by the Russians to re-open communications. Indeed in their policy towards other countries the present leadership seeks to counterbalance what they perceive as the Soviet threat.

The superpower holding the banner of Socialism is the more vicious and expansionist ... it occupied its ally Czechoslovakia by force ... it threatens the security of Western Europe ... its strategy in Asia is to put down a cordon around the continent and with Cuba and Vietnam as the falcon and the hound, to launch a southward offensive from Africa and the Middle East to South East Asia to seek strategic war materials and control the oil supplies. (*Beijing Review*, 1979)

Sino-American relations

In the period of the 'Cold War' and the American policy of the containment of Communism, China regarded America as the arch-enemy. The U.S.A. recognized the Chiang Kai-shek regime as the legitimate government of China, gave substantial economic and military aid to Taiwan, imposed an embargo on all trade with China, and prevented her entry to the United Nations.

With the outbreak of the Korean War in 1950 both countries became involved; China in defence of a friendly neighbour and her own border, America to ensure the future of a democratic South Korea. Likewise in Vietnam the two countries opposed one another. Whilst American troops and finance supported the non-Communist government in South Vietnam, China sent arms and economic aid to the Communists in North Vietnam, Laos and Cambodia.

However, by the late sixties both the United States and China were prepared to consider a new relationship. After their failure in Vietnam the Americans were keen to adopt an alternative strategy. Their own domestic problems and growing unease at Soviet military strength made friendship with China an attractive option. The Sino-Soviet dispute largely explains China's changed attitude. They realized that reconciliation with America would allow them access to western technology, but more importantly they thought it would provide increased security against the threat of Soviet aggression.

Between 1969 and 1971 relations gradually improved. China was admitted to the United Nations in 1971 and after President Nixon's visit to Beijing in 1972 co-operation and trade developed. On 1 January 1979 full diplomatic relations were established between the two countries. The problem of Taiwan, a major sticking-point in the intervening years, is still unsolved. The Americans have withdrawn their military aid and recognized Taiwan as part of mainland China, whilst the Chinese have given assurances that there will be no military take-over.

Despite the normalization of relations, China still regards America as a superpower that maintains 'interests' in other parts of the world. However, it is China's present view that America is not 'expansionist' and is therefore less dangerous than the Soviet Union. Vice-Chairman Deng Xiaoping, in his visit to the United States in 1979, continually stressed the danger to the world of superpower hegemony and called for American participation in a united front to 'curb the polar bear'.

CHINA AND THE SECOND WORLD

Following Sino-American détente, China normalized diplomatic relations with many European nations and Canada, New Zealand, Australia and Japan.

Japan

Both countries have gained substantially from their new relationship. Japan, one of the world's largest manufacturing nations with few indigenous resources of her own, has gained access to China's deposits of oil, minerals and raw materials, and for the Chinese, Japan is a vital source of advanced technology. In the Sino-Japanese Treaty of Peace and Friendship signed in 1978, it was agreed to increase bilateral trade to the value of $20 billion a year by 1985, thus securing Japan's position as China's number one trading partner. However, of crucial importance for the Chinese was the inclusion of the following clause: 'Neither of us seeks hegemony in the Asian or Pacific region or in any other region, and we are each opposed to the efforts of any other country or group of countries to establish such hegemony.' Not surprisingly the Soviet Union has been highly critical of Japan's new friendly relations with China.

Vice-Chairman Deng Xiaoping visiting the Space Centre in Houston in 1979.

Premier Hua with Mrs Thatcher, the Prime Minister, in front of Number 10, Downing Street in 1979.

Western Europe

Shortly before his departure on a tour of France, Germany, Italy and the U.K. in 1979, Chairman Hua stated: 'A strong and united Europe is of great significance in the struggle against hegemony...'

Since the new leadership came to power a large number of new trade agreements have been signed. For example, in 1979 China agreed to buy two nuclear power stations from the French and to increase Sino-French trade eight-fold by 1985. In Britain, Chairman Hua spent much of his time visiting new industrial projects such as British Rail's advanced passenger train and an exhibition of the North Sea oil industry. Under the Sino-British agreement on science and technology it is planned to increase bilateral trade to an annual amount of $10 billion by 1985, and substantial loans have been arranged to enable the Chinese to buy British goods.

However, diplomatic visits and trading agreements also have a political point. The Chinese have been quick to criticize détente and S.A.L.T. negotiations as a possible weakening of America's commitment to Europe and they stress the important unifying and defensive roles of the E.E.C. and N.A.T.O. It is illustrative of the Chinese attitude towards Western European affairs that they welcomed the British Conservative Party's election victory in May 1979. Warming to the anti-Soviet stance taken by Mrs Thatcher, the *Beijing Review* had this to say: 'In foreign affairs their call for stronger unity within Western Europe and for building a strong Britain, gained support from voters who are deeply concerned with the increasing threat of Soviet hegemony.'

Eastern Europe

At the World Communist Conference held in Moscow in 1960, the Sino-Soviet dispute split the Communist world. All of the Eastern European states, with the exception of Albania, sided with Russia. Since then China has maintained diplomatic relations with Eastern European countries but inevitably her attitude towards the Soviet Union has created difficulties.

Recently, however, there have been some changes. Relations between China and Albania have deteriorated, whilst friendship with Romania and Yugoslavia, two Eastern European states that enjoy a substantial measure of independence from the Soviet Union, has increased. Chairman Hua was welcomed by both countries on official State visits in 1978. Yet it was not so long ago that the Chinese regarded Tito as a leading revisionist and described him as 'a dwarf kneeling in the mud attempting to spit upon the giant standing on the mountain'. Today Yugoslavia receives praise not only for its policy of non-alignment with the Soviet Union, but also for its self-determined brand of Communism. The present leadership sees merits in Yugoslavia's economic model and in her success in co-operation with the West. In particular they hope to gain insights into how to absorb western technology relatively cheaply and quickly. An indication of the high regard given to the renewed friendship between China and Yugoslavia was the presence of Chairman Hua at President Tito's funeral in May 1980. The Chinese obviously hope that this show of strength with the new collective leadership will deter any Soviet attempt to threaten Yugoslavia.

CHINA AND THE THIRD WORLD

China first adopted the role of spokesman for the Third World at the Bandung Conference of African and Asian countries in 1955. It was here that Zhou Enlai announced the 'Five Principles' which China believes should govern her relations with other countries: 'mutual respect for territorial integrity and sovereignty, mutual non-aggression, non-interference in each other's internal affairs, equality and mutual benefit, and peaceful co-existence.' Since then China has established relations with a number of African, Asian, South American and Middle Eastern countries and often speaks on their behalf at international gatherings and in the United Nations.

For China, Third World co-operation is an important element in her own foreign policy: 'In opposing superpower hegemony, the Third World is the main force' (Marshal Ye Jianying, 1979). Russian and Cuban activities in Third World countries, for example in Angola, Mozambique and South Yemen, have been severely criticized by China, which sees their claims to aid liberation movements as a covert form of hegemony. China has not been slow to modify her own policies accordingly. Vietnam, for instance, which once enjoyed China's support, is now described as the 'oriental Cuba' and condemned for being a pawn in the Soviets' bid for world domination. China's invasion of Vietnam in 1979, to reduce pressure on the highly unpopular Pol Pot regime in Kampuchea, can be viewed as a measure of the strength of China's anti-Soviet feeling and concern over her own security.

The Soviet occupation of Afghanistan, begun in December 1979, is, for the Chinese, proof of their 'Three Worlds Theory' and a vindication of their policies. Although further developments must be expected, the Americans are clearly equally worried by the Soviet actions and have already agreed to sell military equipment to China. The possibility of defensive co-operation between America, China and Pakistan is currently being discussed.

China sees herself as a Third World country and is keen to export her ideas on development. Some countries, mostly in Africa, impressed by her success in the struggle against poverty and unemployment, have adopted aspects of the Chinese approach. Although China gives a very limited amount of aid, she has been responsible for a number of projects, including, for example, road-building in Somalia, the construction of small industries in Tanzania, canals in Ghana, and the celebrated Tan Zam railway in East Africa.

China's foreign policy in perspective

Since the touchstone of Chinese foreign policy is her fear of Soviet hegemony, her willingness to form alliances with anti-Soviet countries on the basis that 'the enemy of our enemy is our friend' has resulted in some very strange bedfellows. For example, China maintains relations with the extreme right-wing government in Chile—General

Pinochet himself was welcomed in Beijing—and only months before the revolution in Iran, Chairman Hua made an official visit to honour the Shah. As we have already seen, support for the British Conservative Party is justified by its 'opposition to Soviet policy'.

For a Communist country, China's attitude towards liberation movements is likewise curious. Ideologically she is committed to the notion that world revolution is inevitable and to supporting the cause of the proletariat. However, China's interpretation of this part of Marxist theory is that people fighting to liberate themselves must initially 'rely on their own efforts', and the struggle against imperialism must come first. This relieves China of the obligation to help every Communist guerrilla movement, a task which she would find financially crippling, but it also allows her to support national revolutions and governments which are anti-Soviet.

The present leadership is unconcerned with the criticism that its policies arouse. Since 1974 they have argued that a 'Socialist camp' no longer exists, and they are unwilling to name the countries that they consider Socialist other than 'Romania, Yugoslavia, North Korea ... and some others'. Socialist solidarity obviously takes second place to sympathy with the Chinese view.

CHINA NOW

As we have seen, China's development in the period 1949–76 was dominated by two different approaches to the problems of economic, political and social organization; the influences of both the Soviet and Maoist models persist in the policies of the present leadership. Whilst the Maoist ideals of 'serving the Party and the people' and the 'Mass Line' still receive attention, the renewed emphasis on expertise, material incentives and the cultivation of foreign assistance harks back to the style of the 1950s.

The debate as to how the policies of the present leadership might be understood is a continuing one. Whilst some argue that their policies represent a 'third way' and a more balanced approach, others see the latest developments as evidence of a rejection of Maoism and an abandonment of his vision of Socialism. The late Chairman would no doubt have criticized the new economic priorities, the stress on individual rewards and élitist education for widening the 'three great differences', and he might well have been apprehensive about the harmful bourgeois influences that foreign involvement in China may bring.

But the apparent rejection of Maoism by the present leadership does not mean that Mao himself, the symbol of the Communist revolution, is now forgotten. He is still of immense significance to the ordinary Chinese people; indeed many regard him as having been personally responsible for the undoubted benefits and achievements which Communism has brought. This point is recognized by today's leaders: 'Without Mao Zedong Thought there would be no new China today.' Mao is also named as an ideological guide in both the recently-revised State and Party Constitutions.

Nevertheless, since 1976 the campaign to arrest the deification of Mao and to de-mythologize his work has gained momentum. Initially the 'Gang of Four', the extreme Maoists, were accused of having treated Mao Zedong Thought as a religious dogma and having instituted his 'law' without regard for the circumstances. In 1978 and 1979 statements emphasizing the collective nature of the leadership and the need to prevent any one person from assuming a position of unrivalled prominence were obvious, if indirect, attacks on Mao's god-like status. Also, increasing attention was paid to the idea that other important revolutionaries such as Zhou Enlai should be honoured as contributors to the wisdom of Mao Zedong Thought. However, in 1980, with the developing power struggle, the criticism of Mao increased. The re-assessment of Party history from 1958–76, the rehabilitation of Liu Shaoqi and the promotion of Zhao Ziyang, indicate a firm anti-Maoist shift in the leadership. Direct responsibility for the alleged political and economic mismanagement of the years 1966–76 is now placed squarely on Mao's shoulders. He is accused, by name, of having committed 'grave errors of judgment' and having 'acted like a feudal lord and tyrant'.

The future attitude towards Mao will depend on the balance of power in the Chinese leadership. Between 1976 and 1979 it appeared that a working relationship had developed between Hua Guofeng and Deng Xiaoping. The disorder of the post-Cultural Revolution period, the grave weaknesses in the economy and the threat posed by international isolation, all demanded that Hua and Deng maintain Party unity.

Zhao Ziyang, the current Premier of China.

From the start Deng was the senior partner. Hua, a much younger man, was thought to be anxious to maintain unity and to be willing to bide his time. Deng, at 76, has little time to waste and it is due to his energetic leadership that the drive to modernize China and to increase her contacts with the outside world has proceeded so rapidly. However, the events of 1980 suggest that the working relationship between Hua and Deng has broken down and that Hua is very much on the defensive. Deng justifies his approach in simple terms—that unless China modernizes her economy and catches up with the West by the year 2000, she will remain weak, a prey to the aggressive tendencies of expansionist powers and prone to internal political discontent arising from the unfulfilled aspirations of the people. He remarked recently that if the present policies succeeded in improving the living standards of the Chinese people, no one would challenge them. But as one observer noted, the previous policies also succeeded in vastly improving those conditions and 'since equality has been relegated as a target, failure on the economic front could have politically explosive effects.'

At the time of writing, the debate about China's future and the best route for Socialism is proceeding and as events move so rapidly there is undoubtedly more of the story to be revealed. In this short book we have tried to present the framework within which the debate takes place; you must decide for yourself how you view current developments.

Postscript

In January 1981 it was announced that Hua Guofeng intended to resign as Chairman of the Party and that his position would be taken by Hu Yaobang. Aged 65, Hu took part in the Long March and the Liberation wars and after 1949 became First Secretary of the Communist Youth League—a prestigious post because it controls entry to the Party. Hu was denounced during the Cultural Revolution and underwent a period of 'reform through labour' and house arrest. He is known to be strongly sympathetic to the pragmatic views of Deng Xiaoping and Zhao Ziyang and a firm supporter of their modernization policies.

Who's Who

DENG XIAOPING Born in 1904 in Sichuan, Deng joined the C.P.C. in 1920. He was educated in France and Russia. A veteran of the Long March and the Liberation Wars, he held a variety of important posts until 1965, including Secretary General of the Party and Acting Premier. Disgraced during the Cultural Revolution, he re-emerged in 1973 but was again removed from office in 1976. In 1977 Deng was once more rehabilitated and he took up the post of Vice-Premier, a position which he resigned in 1980. He continues as Vice-Chairman of the Party.

HUA GUOFENG Born in 1920 in Shanxi, he was active in the Land Reform movement and became a leading cadre in Hunan in 1959. From 1971 he served under Zhou Enlai in Beijing. In 1976 Hua became Premier and Chairman of the Party. He resigned as Premier in September 1980.

JIANG QING She was born in 1914 in Shandong into a 'middle peasant' family and became a film actress in Shanghai in the 1920s. She went to Yanan to join the C.P.C. and became Mao's fourth wife. Jiang Qing rose to national political prominence during the Cultural Revolution when she organized massive Red Guard demonstrations in support of Mao. After 1968 she was in control of the mass media and responsible for the introduction of revolutionary opera. With her associates Zhang Chunqiao, Wang Hongwen and Yao Wenyuan, she was arrested after Mao's death and denounced as the leader of the 'Gang of Four'. The Gang were put on public trial early in 1981.

LIU SHAOQI Born in 1898 in Hunan into a 'rich peasant' family he joined the C.P.C. in the 1920s, studied in Moscow and was active as a Party organizer of urban workers. By the mid-1940s he was second only to Mao in the Party hierarchy. Throughout the 1950s and 1960s Liu played a leading role in Party and State affairs as Vice-Chairman of the Central Committee. He became Chairman of the P.R.C. in 1959. Liu's 'second-in-command' was Deng Xiaoping. Denounced in 1966 as the 'arch revisionist' and accused of 'taking the Capitalist road', he was expelled from the Party in 1968 and exiled to his home village. Liu died in 1969 and was posthumously rehabilitated in 1980.

ZHAO ZIYANG   Zhao was born in Henan in 1919. He served in the Liberation War and became a leading cadre in Guangdong in the '50s. Disgraced during the Cultural Revolution, Zhao was rehabilitated in 1971 and in 1975 was sent to Sichuan where he became Provincial Party Secretary. In September 1980 Zhao assumed the Premiership.

ZHOU ENLAI   Born in 1898 in Jiangsu into a well-to-do landlord family he was educated in Japan and France. He was active in C.P.C. affairs from 1924. After 1949 he became the chief diplomat in China's dealings with foreign countries and, as Premier from 1954 onwards, the most important administrator in the huge State bureaucracy. Never a rival to Mao, Zhou is credited with restoring order after the Cultural Revolution and unmasking the 'Lin Biao plot'. Acknowledged by the present leadership as the 'father of the Four Modernizations', Zhou died, highly honoured, in 1976.

Glossary of Terms

AUTONOMOUS REGION Province characterized by a substantial national minority presence.

BUREAUCRATISM Officialism, a tendency to follow rules rigidly.

CADRE A Party or State official (literally: backbone personnel).

DAZIBAO Wall poster (literally: a big character poster).

DEMOCRACY WALL A square in Beijing where dazibao were displayed.

DOGMATISM In the Chinese context, used to describe arrogant and assertive attitudes and a willingness to quote political doctrine without applying it to the practical situation.

FEN One hundredth of a yuan.

HEGEMONY Prevailing influence of one state over others.

IDEOLOGY A set of political theories which determines action. In China the ideological guides are the writings of Marx, Lenin and Mao Zedong.

INTERMEDIATE TECHNOLOGY Small-scale machinery ranging from basic tools to relatively sophisticated equipment such as small generators and walking tractors.

JIN Half a kilogramme.

LIBERATION The term the Chinese use to refer to 1949.

MU, MOW One sixth of an acre.

PEASANT The Communist Party analysis of the rural class structure as it existed before 1949 included the following categories:
Labourers: those who owned no land and depended on wages earned by working for others;
Poor peasants: those who rented land and supplemented their income by working for others;
Middle peasants: those who owned part of their land and rented part, and depended on their own labour;
Rich peasants: those who owned enough land for themselves but also hired labour. Some engaged in money-lending;

Landlords: those who owned sizeable amounts of land but did no manual work. Their income was gained through rents, money-lending and other commercial ventures.

In practice the boundaries between classes overlapped.

POLEMICS   The practice or art of controversy.

PRIVATE PLOT   A portion of land for private use which is owned by the individual or household.

REVISIONIST   Technically, someone who has revised Marxism to the point where reform replaces revolution. In China, the term is often used to refer to someone who favours Soviet-style policies.

SCHISTOSOMIASIS   A debilitating snail-borne disease causing emaciation, swelling of the stomach, listlessness, sterility in women and often resulting in death.

SIDE-LINE ACTIVITIES   Activities such as keeping chickens or pigs, carried out by individuals or households for private gain.

SOVIET   In the Chinese context, a Communist-held rural area.

SUZERAINTY   The power of supremacy one state has over another.

YUAN   Approximately 20p.

Further Reading

Books

China, 1949–76 Colin Bown (HEINEMANN, 1977)

Fanshen: Documentary of Revolution in a Chinese village William Hinton (MONTHLY REVIEW PRESS, 1980)

The Chinese Cultural Revolution Adrian Hsia (ORBACH & CHAMBERS, 1972)

Mao Tse-tung Stuart R. Schram (ed.) (PELICAN, 1966)

The Political Thought of Mao Tse-tung Stuart R. Schram (ed.) (PELICAN, 1969)

Mao Tse-tung Unrehearsed Stuart R. Schram (ed.) (PELICAN, 1974)

China Readings Vol. 3 F. Schurmann and O. Schell (eds) (PELICAN, 1971)

China Readings Vol. 4 F. Schurmann and D. & N. Milton (eds) (PELICAN, 1977)

Red Star Over China Edgar Snow (PELICAN, 1972)

Red China Today: The Other Side of the River Edgar Snow (PELICAN, 1971)

Living in China Andrew Watson (BATSFORD, 1975)

Inside China Peter Worsley (ALLEN LANE, 1975)

Periodicals and magazines

China Now Bi-monthly journal of the Anglo-Chinese Educational Institute, London

The China Quarterly Journal of the Contemporary Institute, School of Oriental and African Studies, London

Modern China Booklets from the Anglo-Chinese Institute

P.R.C. PUBLICATIONS IN ENGLISH

Beijing Review (P.O. 399, Beijing) Weekly journal giving Chinese version of political and economic affairs and international relations

China Reconstructs Illustrated monthly journal covering political, economic and cultural affairs